WORKBOO

BIG
ENGLISH 4

Mario Herrera • Christopher Sol Cruz

Big English
Workbook 4

Pearson Education, 10 Bank Street, White Plains, NY 10606 USA

Staff credits: The people who made up the *Big English* team, representing editorial, production, design, manufacturing, and marketing are Rhea Banker, Danielle Belfiore, Carol Brown, Tracey Munz Cataldo, Daniel Comstock, Mindy DePalma, Dave Dickey, Gina DiLillo, Christine Edmonds, Nancy Flaggman, Yoko Mia Hirano, Caroline Kasterine, Amy Kefauver, Lucille Kennedy, Penny Laporte, Christopher Leonowicz, Emily Lippincott, Maria Pia Marrella, Jennifer McAliney, Kate McLoughlin, Julie Molnar, Linda Moser, Kyoko Oinuma, Leslie Patterson, Sherri Pemberton, Pamela Pia, Stella Reilly, Mary Rich, Nicole Santos, Susan Saslow, Donna Schaffer, Chris Siley, Kim Snyder, Heather St. Clair, Mairead Stack, Katherine Sullivan, Jane Townsend, Kenneth Volcjak, and Lauren Weidenman.

Contributing writer: Sarah Bupp

Text composition: Bill Smith Group/Q2A Media

Illustration credits: Q2A Media Services, Matt Latchford, Jamie Pouge

Photo credits: Cover/Title Page (b) KidStock/Blend Images/Glowimages; 2 (cl) Amos Morgan/Getty Images, (cr) KidStock/Blend Images/Getty Images; 3 (tl) Jorg Hackemann/Shutterstock, (tr) David Davis/Shutterstock; (bl) Yuri Arcurs/Shutterstock, (br) Dhoxax/Shutterstock; 5 (tr) Peter Phipp/Travelshots.com/Alamy; 8 (br) Bianca Lavies/National Geographic Image Collection/Getty Images; 9 (tr) Warren Goldswain/Shutterstock; 11 (bl) yalayama/Shutterstock, (br) MBI/Alamy; 12 (tr) Myrleen Pearson/Alamy, (tcr) Radius Images/Glow Images, (c) Sean Locke/iStockphoto, (br) Kidstock/Blend Images/Alamy, (bc) Paul Burns/Tetra Images/Alamy; 13 (t) hartphotography/Shutterstock; 15 (t) Monkey Business Images/Shutterstock; 16 (tr) jjpixs/Fotolia; 17 (cl) yalayama/Shutterstock; 19 (cr) Sonyae/Dreamstime; 20 (c) Monkey Business Images/Dreamstime; 23 (tl) Mark Stout/Fotolia, (tr) Juanmonino/iStockphoto, (tcl) Jonathan Downey/iStockphoto, (tcr) Mark Stout Photography/Shutterstock, (bcl) Eyewave/Dreamstime, (bcr) William Mahar/iStockphoto, (bl) fotogal/Fotolia, (br) aida ricciardiello/Shutterstock; 25 (tr) Blend Images/SuperStock; 28 (t) USDA; 29 (tr) Monkey Business Images/Shutterstock; 30 (cr) Monkey Business Images/Shutterstock; 33 (tl) MSPhotographic/Shutterstock, (tc) Joe Gough/Shutterstock, (tr) Joshua Resnick/Shutterstock, (bl) M. Unal Ozmen/Shutterstock, (br) Fotofermer/Shutterstock; 37 (c) Savannah1969/Dreamstime; 38 (tr) Ivonnewierink/Dreamstime; 39 (tr) Rob Marmion/Shutterstock; 40 (tl) fusebulb/Shutterstock, (tr) nikkytok/Shutterstock, (bl) Sebastian Kaulitzki/Shutterstock, (br) Lebendkulturen.de/Shutterstock; 45 (tl) America/Alamy, (tcl) Jon Berkeley/Alamy, (cl) Lynn M. Stone/naturepl.com, (bcl) The Africa Image Library/Alamy, (bl) haveseen/Fotolia; 48 (tl) jakgree/Fotolia, (tcl) JackF/Fotolia, (bcl) Joel Sartore/National Geographic Image Collection/Getty Images, (bl) Robyn Butler/Shutterstock; 50 (tr) Lenkadan/Shutterstock, (cl) Image Source/Getty Images, (br) Godrick/Dreamstime; 52 (bcl) Jon Berkeley/Alamy, (c) anankkml/Fotolia, (bcr) Robyn Butler/Shutterstock, (bl) Gregory MD./Getty Images, (bc) JackF/Fotolia, (br) Lenkadan/Shutterstock; 53 (tl) Hung Chung Chih/Shutterstock, (tcl) Dr Merlin D Tuttle/Getty Images, (bcl) George Nazmi Bebawl/Shutterstock, (bl) pr2is/Shutterstock; 55 (tl) Robert Landau/Alamy, (tc) GL Archive/Alamy, (tr) PhotoAlto/Alamy, (tcl) Auris/Dreamstime, (tcr) Lucenet Patrice/Oredia Eurl/SuperStock, (cl) Vintage Images/Alamy, (c) ClassicStock/Alamy, (bcl) JazzIRT/iStockphoto, (bcr) Brand Z/Alamy, (bl) ClassicStock/Alamy, (bc) Wave/Glow Images, (br) SuperStock/Glow Images; 60 (tl) Sam Chadwick/Shutterstock, (tc) Pep Roig/Alamy, (tr) Charlie Hutton/Shutterstock; 64 (tl) Shchipkova Elena/Shutterstock, (tcl) Maskot/Glow Images, (tcr) Steve Cukrov/Shutterstock, (tr) eurobanks/Shutterstock, (cl) Ramona Heim/Shutterstock, (c) imagebroker/Alamy, (cr) Auris/Dreamstime, (b) Franck Boston/Fotolia; 65 (bl) Brand Z/Alamy, (br) ClassicStock/Alamy; 67 (bl) Andersen Ross/AgeFotostock, (bc) Blue Jean Images/Alamy, (br) elen_studio/Fotolia; 70 (br) David Page/Alamy; 76 (t) xavier gallego morell/Shutterstock, (b) nicolesy/iStockphoto; 77 (tl) Jacek Chabraszewski/Fotolia, (tc) Anyka/Alamy, (tr) johnrochaphoto/Alamy, (cl) ivan kmit/Fotolia, (c) Peter Albrektsen/Shutterstock, (cr) ameli_k/Fotolia, (bcl) CJPhoto/Fotolia, (bc) AVAVA/Shutterstock, (bcr) clearviewstock/Fotolia, (bl) RF Company/Alamy, (b) Louis-Paul St-Onge/iStockphoto, (br) Kamira/Shutterstock; 86 (c) Iwona Grodzka/Shutterstock, (br) Dave King/DK Images; 87 (singer) Warren Goldswain/Shutterstock, (artist) Stephen Simpson/ZUMA Press/Newscom, (skater) Denis Radovanovic/Shutterstock, (computer) David R. Frazier Photolibrary, Inc./Alamy, (baker) Blend Images/Alamy, (robot) Ian Allenden/123RF, (guitarist) Peter Weber/Shutterstock, (dancer) Alexander Yakovlev/Fotolia; 91 (tc) CREATISTA/Shutterstock, (c) Hunor Kristo/Fotolia, (cr) Greg Wright/Alamy; 93 (tr) ALEX HOFFORD/EPA/Newscom; 94 (tl) Nicemonkey/Shutterstock, (b) Nicemonkey/Shutterstock; 95 (tl) David R. Frazier Photolibrary, Inc./Alamy, (tcl) Denis Radovanovic/Shutterstock, (tcr) Warren Goldswain/Shutterstock, (tr) Stephen Simpson/ZUMA Press/Newscom; 96 (tl) Miflippo/Dreamstime, (bl) Denis Radovanovic/Shutterstock, (br) ameli_k/Fotolia; 97 (tl) Peter Albrektsen/Shutterstock, (tc) johnrochaphoto/Alamy, (bc) David R. Frazier Photolibrary, Inc./Alamy; 102 (tl) Juniors Bildarchiv GmbH/Alamy, (bcr) Rafael Ramirez Lee/Shutterstock, (br) anankkml/Fotolia; 104 (tl) David Page/Alamy, (tr) jjpixs/Fotolia, (bl) elen_studio/Fotolia, (br) Monkey Business/Fotolia; 105 (tl) Bombaert Patrick/Shutterstock, (tc) Ruslan Grumble/Shutterstock, (tr) Dario Sabljak/Shutterstock, (bl) The Africa Image Library/Alamy, (bc) America/Alamy, (br) haveseen/Fotolia; 106 (tl) Denis Radovanovic/Shutterstock, (cr) Peter Weber/Shutterstock

Printed in the United States of America

ISBN-10: 0-13-304509-9
ISBN-13: 978-0-13-3045093

Contents

BIG ENGLISH
♫ Song ♫

From the mountaintops to the bottom of the sea,
From a big blue whale to a baby bumblebee—
If you're big, if you're small, you can have it all,
And you can be anything you want to be!

It's bigger than you. It's bigger than me.
There's so much to do, and there's so much to see!
The world is big and beautiful, and so are we!
Think big! Dream big! Big English!

So in every land, from the desert to the sea,
We can all join hands and be one big family.
If we love, if we care, we can go anywhere!
The world belongs to everyone; it's ours to share.

It's bigger than you. It's bigger than me.
There's so much to do, and there's so much to see!
The world is big and beautiful, and so are we!
Think big! Dream big! Big English!

It's bigger than you. It's bigger than me.
There's so much to do, and there's so much to see!
The world is big and beautiful and waiting for me . . .
    a one, two, three . . .
Think big! Dream big! Big English!

unit 1

Kids in My CLASS

 1 Listen. Write the words in the song.

| bigger | curly | glasses | straight | taller |

♪ **Who's That Girl?**

It's the first day of school,
We're back in our classes.
Everybody looks different—
And I have new ¹ _glasses_ !

Who's that girl
Standing over there?
She's ² _____ than me
And has dark ³ _____ hair.

In my class are the kids I know.
We all change. We all grow.

Wait, I know her.
That's Brenda. She's great!
Last year she was shorter,
And her hair was ⁴ _____.

We're all getting ⁵ _____
Than we were last year.
But some things won't change
Like the friends we make here.

(Chorus)

2 Read and look. Write the names.

Julia wears glasses. She loves art class. She has straight blond hair.

Tony has blond hair. It is a little wavy. He's serious and shy.

Amelia has long black hair. She is funny and likes to talk on the phone.

Jose is friendly and smart. He has brown hair. He likes computers.

1. _____

2. _____

3. _____

4. _____

3 Look at 2. Write *T* for *true* or *F* for *false*.

1. Amelia wears glasses. _____

2. Jose has straight hair. _____

3. Julia has curly hair. _____

4. Tony is friendly. _____

4 What are you like? Write.

_____

5 **Read. Circle the words to complete the sentences.**

1. _____ is a new student.

   a. Amanda   **b.** Cristina

2. _____ and her dad are talking about the new student.

   a. Amanda   **b.** Cristina

3. _____ dark curly hair.

   a. Amanda has   **b.** Cristina has

   c. Amanda and Cristina have

4. _____ has longer hair and is shorter.

   a. Amanda   **b.** Cristina

5. Amanda and Cristina are different in _____.

   a. all ways

   b. some ways

6 **Listen and check (✓).**

1. Ruby is

☐ **a.** taller than Martin's dad.

☐ **b.** shorter than Martin's dad.

2. Philip has

☐ **a.** short hair.

☐ **b.** long hair.

3. Philip likes

☐ **a.** to read and draw.

☐ **b.** to play soccer and baseball.

4. Martin's grandma has

☐ **a.** blue hair.

☐ **b.** brown hair.

5. Martin's grandma

☐ **a.** doesn't wear glasses.

☐ **b.** wears glasses.

7 **Write about your family or friends.**

1. _____ is taller than me.

2. _____'s hair is longer than mine.

3. _____'s hair is curlier than mine.

4. _____ is younger than me.

Grammar

Who is **bigger**, Chris or Tom?	Chris is **bigger than** Tom.

old	→	old**er**
big	→	big**ger**
heavy	→	hea**vier**

8 **Complete the sentences.**

1. Maddie is _____taller_____ than Henry. (tall)

2. Valerie is _____ than I am. (old)

3. My mom's hair is _____ than mine. (curly)

4. My school is _____ than my brother's. (big)

5. This book is _____ than that one. (small)

6. Jon's eyes are _____ than mine. (light)

9 **Look at 8. Copy the sentences. Then complete new sentences.**

1. _____Maddie is taller than Henry._____

   Henry is _____shorter_____ than Maddie.

2. _____Valerie is older than I am._____

   I am _____younger_____ than Valerie.

3. _____

   My hair is _____ than my mom's.

4. _____

   My brother's school is _____ than mine.

5. _____

   That book is _____ than this one.

6. _____

   My eyes are _____ than Jon's.

| My sister's hair is longer than **my hair**. | My sister's hair is longer than **mine**. |
| My sister's hair is longer than **your hair**. | My sister's hair is longer than **yours**. |

10 **Match the meanings.**

1. Bob's friends are older than our friends.   mine
2. Our backpacks are heavier than their backpacks.   yours
3. Your father is smarter than my father.   hers
4. Jose's hair is straighter than his sister's hair.   ours
5. My eyes are darker than your eyes.   theirs

11 **Complete the sentences.**

| hers | mine | ours | theirs | yours |
| shorter | smaller | smarter | taller | younger |

1. **Our dog** is smart, but your dog is very smart.

   Your dog is ___smarter___ than ___ours___.

2. Your class has 12 students. It's small. **Their class** has 15 students.

   Your class is _____ than _____.

3. His cousin is four feet tall. **My cousin** is only three feet tall.

   His cousin is _____ than _____.

4. Juan's hair is short. **Kate's hair** is long.

   Juan's hair is _____ than _____.

5. **Your sister** is 10. His sister is 7.

   His sister is _____ than _____.

12 **Complete the sentences.**

> chance   common   fraternal   identical   triplets

Twins and More

1. A mother gave birth to Maria and Martin together. They don't look alike. They are _____ twins.

2. A mother gave birth to Tina, Gina, and Nina together. They look the same. They are identical _____.

3. A mother gave birth to Bob and Rob together. They look the same. They are _____ twins.

4. Fraternal twins are more _____ than identical twins. Identical twins are very rare.

5. The _____ of having triplets is 1 out of 625 births. Twins are more common.

13 **Read. Circle the answers.**

Multiple Births in Animals

Some scientists say the chance of having identical quadruplets is only 1 in 13 million. Not if you're a nine-banded armadillo! It normally has FOUR identical babies at a time.

Some animals have multiple births, but they aren't always identical. Cats usually give birth to 3–5 kittens and dogs usually have 5–10 puppies.

Some animals rarely or never have multiple births. Elephants only have one baby at a time. Dolphins almost always have only one baby at a time.

1. Nine-banded armadillos always have

a. identical quadruplets.   **b.** fraternal quadruplets.

2. Which animal never has triplets?

a. an elephant   **b.** a cat

3. Which animal almost always has only one baby at a time?

a. a dog   **b.** a dolphin

A paragraph starts with a **topic sentence**. The topic sentence introduces the topic, or the main idea, of the paragraph.

My best friend's name is Gabe.

Detail sentences give details, or information, about the main idea. They come after the topic sentence.

He is taller than me and wears cool glasses.
Gabe is smart, and he is funny, too.
We like to play soccer together on weekends.

A paragraph ends with a **final sentence**. A final sentence talks about the subject again in a different way.

I'm happy to have a friend like Gabe.

14 **Read the paragraph. Circle the detail sentences. Copy the topic and final sentences.**

Mr. Smith is my favorite teacher. He's the music teacher at my school. He can sing! He also plays the piano, the guitar, and the drums. He's really smart, and he is funny. I'm happy to have a teacher like Mr. Smith.

Topic sentence: _____

_____

Final sentence: _____

_____

15 **Write about a favorite teacher.**

Topic sentence: _____

Detail 1: _____

Detail 2: _____

Detail 3: _____

Closing sentence: _____

16 **Listen. Number the pictures.**

17 **Look at 16. Write sentences for the pictures.**

Can I help you?   You can go first.
You dropped something.   You can have a turn.

1. _____

2. _____

3. _____

4. _____

18 **Look at the picture. Then complete the sentences.**

brown	straight
funny	taller
glasses	wavy
serious	younger

1. Mom's hair is _____.

2. Dad's hair is _____.

3. Mia is _____ than Tim.

4. Tim is _____ than Mia.

5. Mia likes to read. She doesn't like jokes. She is _____.

6. Tim likes to tell jokes. He is _____.

7. Grandma has _____ hair and _____.

19 **Rewrite the sentences.**

My hair is longer than yours.

His hair is shorter than mine.

1. **My hair** is longer than yours.
Your hair is shorter
than _____*mine*_____.

2. **His hair** is curlier than hers.
Her hair is straighter
than _____.

3. **Our car** is newer than theirs.
Their car is older
than _____.

4. **Your brother** is taller than mine.
My brother is shorter
than _____.

5. **Her sister** is older than his.
His sister is younger
than _____.

6. **Their house** is smaller than ours.
Our house is bigger
than _____.

unit 2 Our SCHEDULE

 1 Listen and write the words in the song. Then match.

> feed and walk   Make my bed   recycling   set the table   watch a movie

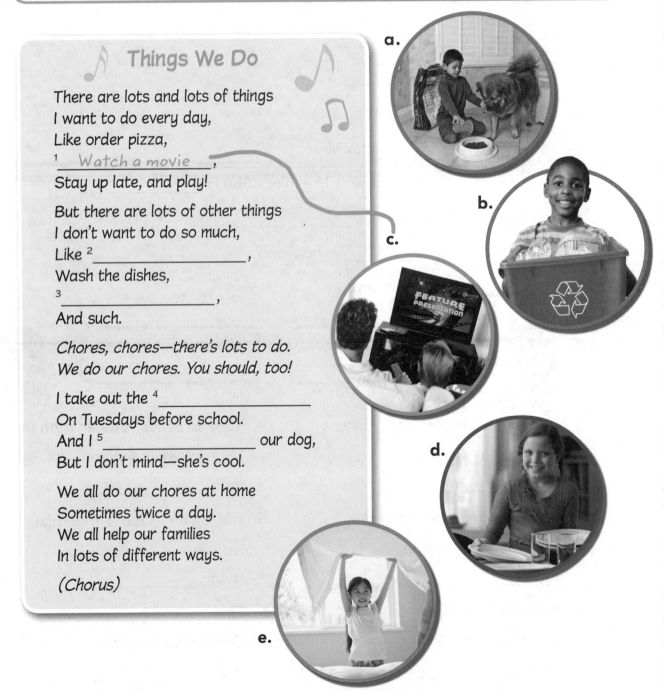

Things We Do

There are lots and lots of things
I want to do every day,
Like order pizza,
¹ _Watch a movie_,
Stay up late, and play!

But there are lots of other things
I don't want to do so much,
Like ² _____,
Wash the dishes,
³ _____,
And such.

Chores, chores—there's lots to do.
We do our chores. You should, too!

I take out the ⁴ _____
On Tuesdays before school.
And I ⁵ _____ our dog,
But I don't mind—she's cool.

We all do our chores at home
Sometimes twice a day.
We all help our families
In lots of different ways.

(Chorus)

a.

b.

c.

d.

e.

2 **Listen and circle.**

1. I brush my teeth twice a **morning / day**.

2. I walk the dog every **week / afternoon**.

3. We walk to school every **morning / day**.

4. We visit our grandparents every **winter / month**.

5. We go skiing every **week / winter**.

6. I take dance lessons once a **morning / week**.

3 **What about you? Complete the chart.**

once a day	twice a day	every night	every summer
I _____	I _____	I _____	I _____
_____	_____	_____	_____
_____	_____	_____	_____
_____	_____	_____	_____
_____	_____	_____	_____
_____	_____	_____	_____
_____	_____	_____	_____
_____	_____	_____	_____

4 **Read. Then answer the questions.**

A Lot of Cousins

1. What are Bradley and Kim talking about?

   _____

2. How often does Kim go to weddings?

   _____

3. Does Kim look excited about weddings?

   _____

4. How many cousins does Kim have?

   _____

5 **What happens next in the story? Write.**

_____

_____

_____

6 **Listen. Complete the sentences.**

1. Mindy and her dad are going to the supermarket Saturday _____.

2. Julian and Billy are going to the movies _____ afternoon.

3. Jenna sees her cousins four _____ a year.

4. Suzanne has soccer practice three times a _____.

5. Joey walks his dog _____ a day.

7 **Read and match.**

1. What are you doing this weekend?

a. About once a week.

2. How often do you eat pizza?

b. They're going to the zoo.

3. Where are they going this afternoon?

c. I'm going to the movies.

Grammar

Where is	he/she	going after school?	He/She	is going to soccer practice.
What are	you	doing tonight?	I	am watching a movie at home.
			We	are watching a movie at home.
	they		They	

8 **Circle the correct word.**

1. **What / Where** are they doing after school?

2. **What / Where** is she doing tomorrow?

3. **What / Where** are they going this summer?

4. **What / Where** is he doing after school?

5. **What / Where** are you doing Saturday morning?

6. **What / Where** are we going on vacation?

9 **Look at the questions in 8. Write the answers.**

1. They're _____going_____ on vacation.

2. She's _____ her cousins.

3. They're _____ to Australia.

4. He's _____ soccer in the park.

5. I'm _____ my room.

6. We're _____ to China.

> cleaning
> going
> going
> going
> playing
> visiting

10 **Answer about you.**

1. What are you doing this weekend?

   _____

2. Where are you going after school?

   _____

How often does	he/she	have guitar lessons?	Once a week. Twice a day. Every Friday. On Sundays. Once a month. Every summer.
How often do	you	go to the dentist?	
	they		

11 **Look at Laura's schedule. Answer the questions.**

This is my schedule.

every day	twice a day
once a week	twice a week

	Sun	Mon	Tue	Wed	Thu	Fri	Sat
play outside	✗	✗	✗	✗	✗	✗	✗
brush teeth	✗✗	✗✗	✗✗	✗✗	✗✗	✗✗	✗✗
help with laundry					✗		
have piano lessons		✗		✗			

1. How often does Laura play outside? _____

2. How often does Laura brush her teeth? _____

3. How often does Laura help her parents with the laundry? _____

4. How often does Laura have piano lessons? _____

12 **Write questions beginning with *How often*.**

1. _How often do_ _____ you go shopping?

2. _____ they play soccer?

3. _____ he eat pizza?

4. _____ you watch TV?

5. _____ she make her bed?

13 **Complete the sentences.**

1. Jenny is _____. She has lots of friends.

2. Paul is _____. He's really handsome.

3. A _____ is a short song.

4. Miss Lulu is a _____ singer. Everyone knows her.

> attractive
> famous
> jingle
> popular

14 **Look at the advertisement. Read the questions and check (✓) the answers.**

1. What tools does this advertisement use?
   - ☐ Characters
   - ☐ Famous People
   - ☐ Slogans and Jingles
   - ☐ Design

2. What does the advertisement say about 123Juice?
   - ☐ It makes you happy.
   - ☐ It makes you popular.
   - ☐ It makes you attractive.
   - ☐ It makes you look younger.

Sequence words tell the order in which things happen. Here are some examples:

My Day at School

First, we have a math lesson.
Next, we have a spelling test.
Then we have lunch.
After that, we have a social studies lesson.
Finally, we have a reading lesson.

Use *first* for the first activity. Use *finally* for the last activity. For the activities in between, you can use the sequence words in any order.

15 **Read the paragraph. Write the sequence words from the box above.**

I am busy after school. _____, I have a
(1)
snack. _____ I walk my dog.
(2)
_____, I play outside. _____,
(3)   (4)
I do my homework. _____, I eat dinner.
(5)

16 **What do you do after school? Add two activities. Then number the activities in order. Write a paragraph.**

_____ do homework   _____ have a snack   _____

_____ eat dinner   _____ play games   _____

I am busy after school. _____

_____

_____

_____

_____

17 Complete the sentences to show good habits and bad habits.
Use words from the box.

| after | always | candy | day | every day |
| month | never | once a week | vegetables | watch TV |

Good Habits	Bad Habits
1. I eat _____ every day.	**1.** I eat _____ every day.
2. I _____ clean my room.	**2.** I _____ clean my room.
3. I exercise _____.	**3.** I exercise _____.
4. I brush my teeth twice a _____.	**4.** I brush my teeth twice a _____.
5. I do my homework _____ school.	**5.** I _____ for four hours after school.

18 What are your habits? Write.

Good habits: _____

_____

Bad habits: _____

_____

19 **Complete the dialogue.**

> After that   doing   First   going   What   Where

Ana: Hey, José! _____ are you doing after school?

José: I'm really busy. _____, I'm visiting my grandmother.

Ana: Then what are you _____?

José: Then I'm meeting my mom.

Ana: _____ are you going?

José: We're _____ to the dentist.

Ana: Oh, too bad.

José: That's okay. _____, we're going to the movies!

20 **Complete the questions. Then write answers. Use words from the box.**

> go on vacation/twice a year   play outside/every day
> wash dishes/twice a week   watch a movie/twice a week

1.
How often _does he wash dishes_____?

He _____

2.
How often _____?

_____

3.
How often _____?

_____

4.
How often do they _____?

_____

unit 3

I Like to EAT!

 1 Listen and write the words in the song. Then match.

♪ **Try Something New** ♪

"Hey there, Sam, try something new.
Just take a little bite and chew.
Now's your chance. Please don't waste it.
You won't know if you like it till you taste it."

"Would you like some ¹_____?
Tonight it tastes especially nice!"
Sam says, "No, Dad, not right now.
But thanks so much—thanks, anyhow."

Come on, Sam, please take a little taste!
Come on, Sam, don't make a funny face!

"How about a ²_____?
It's really yummy. Come on, try one!"
Sam says, "No, Dad, not right now.
But thanks so much—thanks, anyhow."

"Would you like some ³_____?"
"No thanks, Dad. I'm in a hurry!"
"How about a ⁴_____?"
"No thanks, Dad. Later! See ya!"

(Chorus)

"Come on, Sam. Just one little bite!"
"Oh my gosh, Dad. Oh, all right!
Mmm. Hey, you're right. It's great!
Please put some more on my plate!"

a. chicken curry

b. corn tortilla

c. beef fried rice

d. sweet steamed bun

2 Match. Write the letter.

	a.	e.	
1. __d__ oatmeal			**5.** _____ pasta with vegetables
	b.	**f.**	
2. _____ yogurt with fruit			**6.** _____ eggs in tortillas
	c.	**g.**	
3. _____ a grilled cheese sandwich			**7.** _____ cereal with milk
	d.	**h.**	
4. _____ rice and beans			**8.** _____ noodle soup

3 What food do you like?

Breakfast _____

Lunch _____

Dinner _____

4 **Read. Then write *T* for *true* or *F* for *false*.**

1. "It's, uh…good" means Patty really likes Theo's lemonade. _____

2. Patty says Theo's lemonade tastes terrible. _____

3. Theo put sugar in the lemonade. _____

4. Theo forgot to put sugar in the lemonade. _____

5. The lemonade tastes sweet. _____

5 **What happens next in the story? Write.**

_____

_____

_____

_____

6 **Listen. Check (✓) the answers.**

1. Pablo would like

☐ **a.** chicken fried rice.

☐ **b.** rice and beans.

☐ **c.** pizza.

2. The vegetable curry is

☐ **a.** salty.

☐ **b.** sour.

☐ **c.** spicy.

3. Grandma would like

☐ **a.** yogurt with fruit and sugar.

☐ **b.** yogurt with fruit.

☐ **c.** fruit with sugar.

4. Anna-Marie thinks the corn tortillas are

☐ salty.   ☐ spicy.   ☐ sweet.

5. The girl likes

☐ orange juice.   ☐ lemonade.   ☐ water.

7 **Answer about you.**

1. I like food that is

☐ salty.   ☐ sour.   ☐ spicy.   ☐ sweet.

2. What would you like for dinner?

I'd like _____.

Grammar

What **would** you **like**?		**I'd like** some soup.		I'd like ⟶ I would like
What **would**	he/she	**like**?	He**'d**/She**'d** **like** yogurt.	He'd/She'd like ⟶ He/She would like

8 Listen and check (✓). Then complete the sentences.

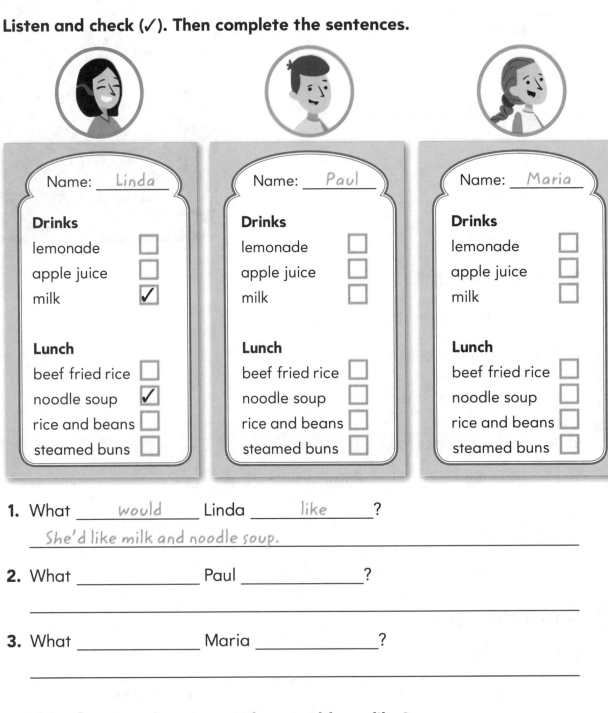

Name: _Linda_

Drinks
- lemonade ☐
- apple juice ☐
- milk ☑

Lunch
- beef fried rice ☐
- noodle soup ☑
- rice and beans ☐
- steamed buns ☐

Name: _Paul_

Drinks
- lemonade ☐
- apple juice ☐
- milk ☐

Lunch
- beef fried rice ☐
- noodle soup ☐
- rice and beans ☐
- steamed buns ☐

Name: _Maria_

Drinks
- lemonade ☐
- apple juice ☐
- milk ☐

Lunch
- beef fried rice ☐
- noodle soup ☐
- rice and beans ☐
- steamed buns ☐

1. What _____would_____ Linda _____like_____?
   She'd like milk and noodle soup.

2. What _____ Paul _____?
   _____

3. What _____ Maria _____?
   _____

9 Look at **8**. Write about you. What would you like?

_____

Would	you he/she they	like to try some curry?	Yes,	I we he/she they	would.	No,	I we he/she they	wouldn't.

10 **Look at the pictures. Complete the sentences.**

1.

A: ___Would___ she ___like___
to have some pasta?

B: ___No___, she ___wouldn't___.

2.

A: _____ he _____
to eat some oatmeal?

B: _____, he _____.

3.

A: _____ they _____
to drink mango smoothies?

B: _____, they _____.

4.

A: _____ they _____
to try some curry?

B: _____, they _____.

11 **Write about you.**

1. _____ you _____ to try _____?
Yes, I _____.

2. _____ you _____ to try _____?
No, I _____.

A Balanced Diet

12 Write food on the My Plate chart for a balanced diet.

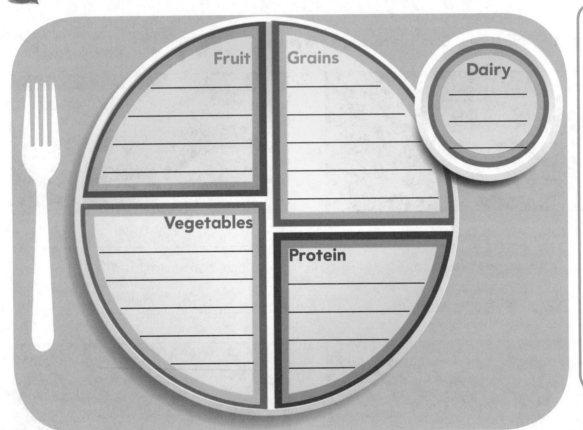

Fruit	Grains	Dairy
Vegetables	Protein	

banana
beef
bread
broccoli
carrots
cereal
cheese
chicken
mango
milk
orange
pasta
peppers
spinach
rice
tofu
yogurt

13 Label food Taro and Lisa eat. Who has a balanced diet? Circle *Taro* or *Lisa*.

D = Dairy   F = Fruit   G = Grain   P = Protein   V = Vegetable

Taro eats . . .

_D, G_ cereal with milk.
_____ a banana.
_____ some strawberries.
_____ a chicken sandwich.
_____ a salad.
_____ yogurt.
_____ tofu.
_____ rice.

Lisa eats . . .

_G_ bread.
_____ cheese.
_____ yogurt.
_____ beef fried rice.
_____ carrots.
_____ potato chips.
_____ chicken.
_____ pasta.

14 **Read. Then write about *your* school lunches. What is the same? What is different?**

School Lunches

What do they eat for lunch in Brazil?

Japan	_____ (my country)	Same or Different?
Kids take turns serving.	We bring lunch from home.	different
Kids eat lunch in their classroom.		
Brazil		
Rice and beans are always part of the meal.		
Lunch is bigger than breakfast or dinner.		
Zambia		
People often eat the same thing for lunch and dinner.		
People eat some food with their hands.		
Italy		
Food is organic, or grown naturally.		
Kids eat meat for lunch once or twice a week.		

Use conjunctions such as *and*, *but*, and *or* to join two sentences into one sentence.

I eat breakfast at home. Then I walk to school.
→ I eat breakfast at home, <u>and</u> then I walk to school.

Dad eats a big breakfast. Mom has only toast.
→ Dad eats a big breakfast, <u>but</u> Mom has only toast.

We can eat dinner at home. We can go to a restaurant.
→ We can eat dinner at home, <u>or</u> we can go to a restaurant.

15 **Match and circle the conjunctions.**

1. She doesn't like milk,

2. I usually eat a sandwich for lunch,

3. Would you like pizza,

4. We can have a picnic,

5. Mark doesn't like apples,

6. I eat a balanced diet,

a. or we can eat at my house.

b. and I exercise every day.

c. but today I'm having soup.

d. and his sister doesn't like oranges.

e. 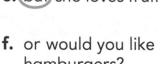 but she loves fruit.

f. or would you like hamburgers?

16 **Join the sentences and write. Use *and*, *but*, or *or*.**

1. We eat lunch in my classroom. We all help clean up.

_____

2. Do you eat a big lunch? Do you eat a big dinner?

_____

3. Carla usually doesn't eat vegetables. Today she's having salad.

_____

17 **Write questions or answers.**

1. What would she like for breakfast?

_____

2. _____?
He'd like a grilled cheese sandwich for lunch.

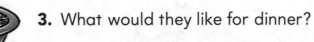

3. What would they like for dinner?

_____

4. _____?
They'd like chicken curry for dinner.

? **5.** What would you like for dinner?

_____

18 **Complete the dialogue. Write _would_ or _wouldn't_.**

Mom: _____ you like to go to the Indian restaurant?

Bobby: No, I _____.

Mom: _____ you like to go to the Italian restaurant?

Bobby: No, I _____.

Mom: _____ you like to go to the Korean restaurant?

Bobby: No, I _____.

Mom: Where _____ you like to go for dinner?

Bobby: How about the candy store?

1 Choose and draw one path. Design a robot.

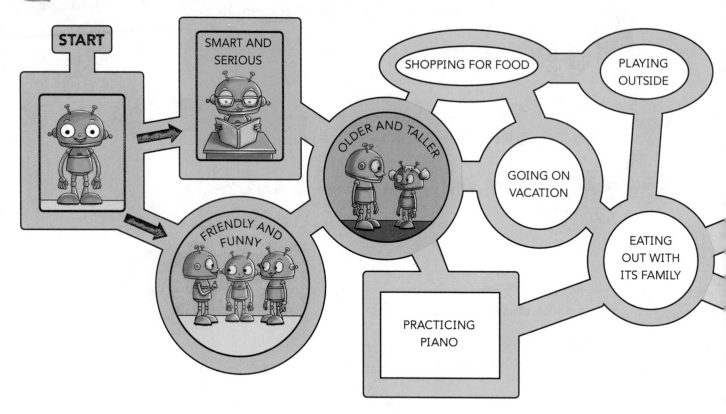

START

SMART AND SERIOUS

SHOPPING FOR FOOD

PLAYING OUTSIDE

OLDER AND TALLER

GOING ON VACATION

FRIENDLY AND FUNNY

EATING OUT WITH ITS FAMILY

PRACTICING PIANO

2 Look at your path in **1**. Answer the questions with words from your path.

What is the robot like? _____

What is it doing today? _____

What would it like to try? _____

3 Look at your path in **1**. Check (✓) the word or words.

My robot likes ☐ spicy ☐ salty ☐ sweet ☐ sour food.

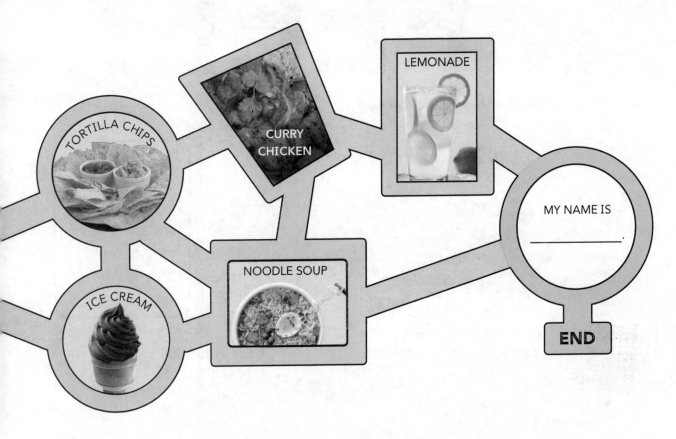

4 Look at the information about your robot. Give it a name. Write a paragraph about your robot.

_____

_____

_____

_____

_____

_____

5 In Your Classroom

Work in a group and share.

unit 4

How Do You FEEL?

1 Listen and write the words in the song.

Stay in Bed and Rest!

You're ¹ _____, and you're ² _____.
You need to stay in bed.
I think you have a fever.
Here, let me feel your head.
You shouldn't go to school today.
You should ³ _____ instead.

When you're sick or feeling blue,
Your family takes good care of you.

You have a ⁴ _____ and a ⁵ _____.
Here's what I suggest:
You should drink some ⁶ _____ and juice.
⁷ _____ and rest!
Listen to your dad now
Because your dad knows best.

(Chorus)

cold
coughing
fever
sneezing
stay home
Stay in bed
tea

2 Read and circle.

When you're sick, here's what I suggest:

1. You shouldn't
   a. stay in bed.
   b. go to school.
   c. stay home.

2. You shouldn't
   a. run around.
   b. rest.
   c. drink water.

3. You shouldn't
   a. go to a doctor.
   b. drink soda and eat candy.
   c. take care of yourself.

3 **Complete the sentences.**

allergies   coughing   fever   headache
scrape   sneezing   sore throat   stomachache

1. My mom has bad `a` `(l)` `l` `e` `r` `g` `i` `e` `s` .

2. Her eyes are watering and she's ○□□□□□○□ .

3. I have a cold. I'm □□`(u)`□○□□ and I feel tired.

4. I have a really bad □□□□○□□□□□□ .
   I don't want to eat anything.

5. Your dad has a □□□□□○□□ . Please turn off the TV.

6. My little sister fell. Now she has a bad □□□□□`(P)`□ on her leg.

7. Grandma has a bad □□□○□□□□□□ . She's
   drinking tea.

8. Your head feels hot. You must have a □□□○□ .

4 **Write the letters from the circles in 3. Use the letters to complete the joke.**

`(l)` ○ ○ `(u)` ○ ○ ○ `(P)` ○ ○

Doctor, my son
ate my pen! What
should I do?

`(u)` ○ ○ ○
`(P)` ○ ○ ○ ○ `(l)`

Story

5 **Read. Then answer the questions.**

1. Paul sees Emma's arm. How does he feel?

   _____

2. Where does Paul think Emma should go?

   _____

3. What does Paul think Emma should do?

   _____

4. What does Emma try to tell Paul?

   _____

6 **What happens next? Write.**

   _____

   _____

7 **Listen and match.**

1. Michael's dad thinks he should   **a.** headache.

2. Vicky should   **b.** take better care of herself.

3. Jinsoo has a bad   **c.** takes good care of himself.

4. Emily's big sister should   **d.** have some crackers.

5. Dennis's grandfather   **e.** allergies.

6. Sally has   **f.** lie down and rest.

8 **Read the dialogue. Circle *T* for *true* or *F* for *false*.**

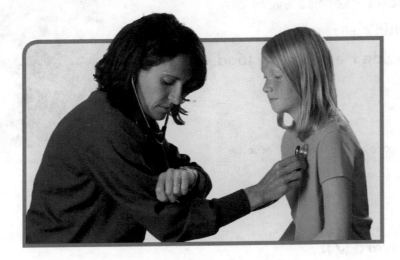

Nurse:	What's the matter, Jessica?
Jessica:	I don't feel good.
Nurse:	Let me check you out.
Jessica:	My tooth hurts.
Nurse:	Oh! You should take some medicine.
Jessica:	OK. That's all?
Nurse:	No, you should see a dentist.

1. Jessica has a stomachache.   **T**   **F**

2. Jessica has a toothache.   **T**   **F**

3. The nurse thinks Jessica is sick.   **T**   **F**

4. Jessica should go to the dentist.   **T**   **F**

I			I	
You			You	
He/She	**should** eat healthy foods.		He/She	**shouldn't** stay up late.
We			We	
They			They	

9 **Circle *should* or *shouldn't*.**

1. I **should / shouldn't** eat more vegetables.
2. You **should / shouldn't** drink so much soda.
3. He **should / shouldn't** exercise every day.
4. We **should / shouldn't** stay up late.
5. They **should / shouldn't** eat healthy food.

I		**myself**.
You		**yourself**.
He/She	should take care of	**himself/herself**.
We		**ourselves**.
They		**themselves**.

10 **Choose the correct word (✓).**

1. I go to bed late and eat potato chips. I should take better care of _____.

   ☐ myself ☐ yourself ☐ herself

2. You never eat fruit. You should take better care of _____.

   ☐ myself ☐ yourself ☐ ourselves

3. She doesn't exercise. She should take better care of _____.

   ☐ himself ☐ themselves ☐ herself

4. We eat a lot of sweets. We should take better care of _____.

   ☐ myself ☐ ourselves ☐ themselves

5. They watch TV all the time. They should take better care of _____.

   ☐ themselves ☐ ourselves ☐ herself

11 **Write should or shouldn't.**

1. **Joe:** I have a headache.

   Doctor: You ____should____ take some medicine.

2. **Mom:** My daughter has a sore throat.

   Doctor: She _____ take care of herself.

3. **Tim:** I'm really tired.

   Doctor: You _____ stay up so late.

4. **Dad:** My children have allergies.

   Doctor: They _____ stay inside and take medicine.

5. **Mom:** My son has a fever.

   Doctor: He _____ go to school.

6. **Sonya:** I like to watch TV for hours every day.

   Doctor: You _____ watch so much TV.

12 **Read the problems. Write advice.**

1. I'm coughing, and I have a sore throat.

   _____

2. My brother has a scrape on his leg.

   _____

3. My friends don't eat vegetables.

   _____

4. I have a stomachache.

   _____

5. I have a fever.

   _____

13 **Read. Then write the answers.**

About Germs
1. very small
2. take away our energy
3. make a poison called a "toxin"
4. toxins cause sickness

Where to Find Germs
1. sink
2. toothbrush
3. remote control
4. computer keyboard
5. bathtub

Germs

BACTERIA

FUNGI

Types of Germs
1. bacteria
2. fungi
3. protozoa
4. viruses

PROTOZOA

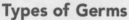

VIRUS

How to Protect Ourselves
1. wash hands
2. keep the house clean

1. What are the four types of germs?

_____

2. How big are germs?

_____

3. What do germs make?

_____

4. Name some places at home where you can find germs.

_____

5. Name some places at school where you can find germs.

_____

6. How can you protect yourself from germs?

_____

Use a comma before conjunctions such as *and*, *but*, and *or* when joining two sentences into one sentence.

> I eat good food. I exercise every day.
> → I eat good food, and I exercise every day.

> My sister likes sweets. She doesn't eat them every day.
> → My sister likes sweets, but she doesn't eat them every day.

> We can take a walk in the park. We can watch some TV.
> → We can take a walk in the park, or we can watch some TV.

Use commas to separate items in a list.

> I like walking in the park, riding my bicycle, listening to music, watching movies, and shopping.

14 **Add commas where they belong in the sentences.**

1. I get lots of rest and I drink plenty of water.

2. I should eat more fruit but I don't like it.

3. Should I watch TV or should I do my homework?

4. The four types of germs are bacteria fungi protozoa and viruses.

5. You should drink some tea and you should take some medicine.

6. I have a toothache but I don't want to go to the dentist.

15 **Write answers. Remember to use commas.**

1. I want to eat a healthy lunch. What should I eat?

_____

_____

2. I want to be healthy and exercise. What should I do?

_____

_____

3. I have a stomachache and a fever. What should I do?

_____

_____

16 **Read and write advice for good hygiene.**

You see, I have a terrible cold . . . achoo!

1. Adam has a bad cold and coughs a lot.
What should he do?

_____

2. Jason and Maggie just came in from playing outside.
What should they do before eating a snack?

_____

3. Carol wants to share her ice cream.
What should her friend do?

_____

4. Tomas has a fever at school.
What should he do?

_____

5. Suzie took out the trash.
What should she do before dinner?

_____

6. Peggy's spoon fell on the floor.
What should she do?

_____

17 **Look. Complete the sentences. Then match.**

| allergies | fever | headache | scrape | sore throat | stomachache |

1. She has a ___headache___ .   **a.** He needs a bandage.

2. He has a _____ .   **b.** She should stay inside.

3. She has a _____ .   **c.** He should drink some tea.

4. He has a _____ .   **d.** She should stay in bed and rest.

5. She has _____ .   **e.** He shouldn't eat sweets.

6. He has a _____ .   **f.** She should take some medicine.

18 **Complete the sentences.**

What should you do to take care of yourself?

You should _____ .

You shouldn't _____ .

Weird and Wild
ANIMALS

1 Listen and read. Then draw animals.

Understanding Animals

Do you know a lot about animals and
All the different types there are?
Some are big, and some are small,
And some are just bizarre!

Understanding animals is good for us to do.
Learning about animals helps us and helps them, too!

Some live in trees or in the sea,
And some live where it's hot.
Some are beautiful, and some are cute,
And some are . . . well, they're not!

(Chorus)

It's important to learn about animals,
Though many seem strange, it's true.
When we learn about animals,
We learn about ourselves, too.

(Chorus)

2 Write the animals.

big	small	live in trees	live in the sea
elephant	frog	monkey	sea lion

3 **Write the names of the animals. Then match.**

| angler fish   Angora rabbit   coconut crab   tarsier   whistling spider |

1. _____

2. _____

3. _____

4. _____

5. _____

a. It has long, sharp teeth. It's from deep oceans all over the world.

b. It has big eyes. Its body is about 10 centimeters (cm) long and its tail is 25 centimeters (cm) long.

c. It has sharp claws. It lives on many islands in the ocean.

d. It has long, soft fur. It weighs about 4 kilograms (kg).

e. It has eight legs. It's about 22 centimeters (cm) wide.

4 **Read. Then answer the questions.**

Chimps Are Smart!

Erika and her brother Adam are watching a TV show about chimpanzees. Chimps are smart and amazing animals. They use their bodies and voices to talk to other chimps. Some chimps can use sign language. They know how to make tools. They use tools to get food in the jungle. Adam can't open his bag of chips. He wonders whether chimps can open bags of chips.

1. Write two amazing things about chimps.

_____

_____

2. Chimps use tools to get food. What tools do you use to get food?

_____

3. Some chimps can use sign language. Do you think they are smart?

_____

4. Where did Erika get her information about chimps?

_____

5. What problem does Adam have?

_____

6. What tool could help Adam?

_____

15

5 Listen. Complete the sentences.

200	fur
3,000	habitats
bats	pandas
endangered	pets
fish	tortoises

1. Bumblebee _____ are endangered.
   There are only _____ left.
   Farmers burn trees where they live.

2. There are only about _____ tigers left in the world. There were more
   tigers, but people kill them for their _____ and to make medicine.

3. Red _____ come from China and the Himalayas. They are
   _____ because people are cutting down the trees where they live.

4. There were over 50,000 Egyptian _____ in the wild. Now there are
   only about 7,500 because people keep them as _____.

5. Mexican walking _____ are almost extinct. They live in streams
   and ponds, but their _____ are polluted.

6 Write the animal's name. Why is each animal endangered? Match.

a.

1. _____

b.

c.

2. _____

3. _____

d.

4. _____

Grammar

How many chimpanzees were there 100 years ago?	There **were** more than one million. But now there **are** only about 200,000.

7 **Read the chart. Then complete the dialogues.**

		There were . . .	There are . . .
	Komodo dragon	How many? *more than 20,000* When? *fifty years ago*	How many? *fewer than 5,000* When? *now*
	Andean condor	How many? *many* When? *in the past*	How many? *a few thousand* When? *now*
	volcano rabbit	How many? *1,000* When? *fifty years ago*	How many? *probably a few hundred* When? *now*
	Tasmanian devil	How many? *100,000* When? *twenty-five years ago*	How many? *20,000* When? *now*

1. **A:** ___*How many*___ | *volcano rabbits* | ___*were there*___ fifty years ago?

   B: ___*There were*___ 1,000. Now ___*there are*___ probably a few hundred.

2. **A:** _____ | | _____ in the past?

   B: _____ many. Now _____ only a few thousand.

3. **A:** _____ | | _____ fifty years ago?

   B: _____ more than 20,000. Now _____ fewer than 5,000.

4. **A:** _____ | | _____ twenty-five years ago?

   B: _____ 100,000. Now _____ 20,000.

Why are chimpanzees endangered?	They're endangered **because** people are moving into their habitat.

8 Why are they endangered? Follow each maze. Then complete the dialogues.

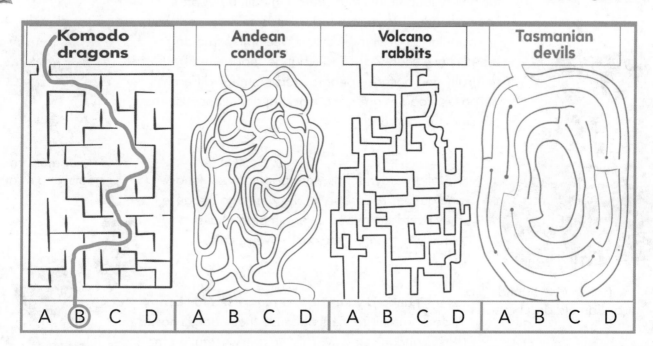

A = There is too much pollution.   C = People are moving into their habitat.
B = People are killing them.   D = They are getting sick and dying.

1. **A:** _____Why_____ are Komodo dragons endangered?

   B: They're endangered _____because_____ | people are killing them |.

2. **A:** _____ are Andean condors endangered?

   B: They're endangered _____ | |.

3. **A:** _____ are volcano rabbits endangered?

   B: They're endangered _____ | |.

4. **A:** _____ are Tasmanian devils endangered?

   B: They're endangered _____ | |.

9 **Read. Then circle _T_ for _true_ or _F_ for _false_.**

People's Best Friend

People have enjoyed keeping domestic dogs as pets for a very long time. Dogs are often called people's "best friends." There are many kinds of dogs and they are popular all over the world. Over time some dog breeds have changed. These changes happened both naturally and because people bred them for different purposes. Poodles are good working dogs, because they are smart and strong.

Poodles are
smart and strong.

Italian Greyhounds
are an old dog breed.

Italian Greyhounds were popular with kings and queens in Europe a long time ago because they could warm beds. People didn't have electricity then, so the castles were cold!

A hundred years ago farmers used to like Jack Russell Terriers because these dogs chased rats and mice away. This was very useful on the farm. Jack Russell Terriers are small, but they are one of the most hard-working breeds.

Jack Russell Terriers
are very hard-working.

1. Poodles are smart dogs.   T   F
2. Italian Greyhounds are a new breed.   T   F
3. Jack Russell Terriers are not hard-working.   T   F
4. Dog breeds never change.   T   F

10 **Which dog would you like as a pet? Explain.**

_____

_____

_____

Dragons

11 **Listen and circle the correct words.**

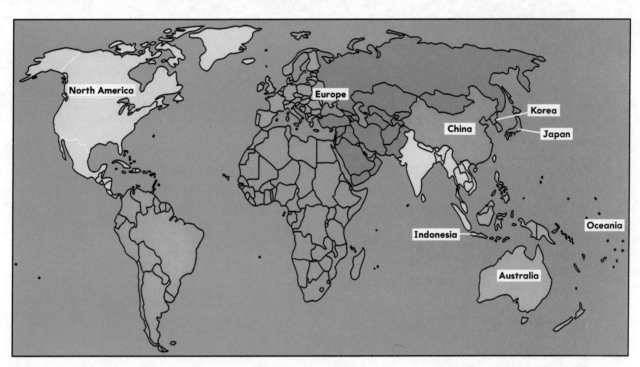

1. In North America and Europe, dragons are
   - **good** / **evil**
   - **fire-breathing** / **real**
   - **funny** / **scary**

2. In China, Japan, and Korea, dragons are
   - beautiful and **magical** / **evil**
   - **winged** / **helpful**
   - **scary** / **not scary**

3. In Oceania and Australia, dragons are
   - called **Western** / **Bunyip**
   - **friendly** / **scary**
   - made of different parts of **animals** / **people**

4. In Indonesia, dragons are
   - **real** / **mythical**
   - **large lizards** / **birds**
   - **extinct** / **endangered**

A sentence may end with a period (.), a question mark (?), or an exclamation point (!). These are called end marks.

Use a period at the end of a sentence that makes a statement.
   I like stories about dragons.

Use a question mark at the end of a direct question.
   Do you have a pet?

If you want a statement to show strong feeling, use an exclamation point at the end.
   The whistling spider is scary!

12 **Write a period, a question mark, or an exclamation point.**

1. How many chimps were there 100 years ago____

2. Angler fish live in deep oceans all over the world____

3. Wow____ That frog is so amazing____

13 **Write sentences. Include a period, a question mark, or an exclamation point.**

1.
angler fish
Angler fish have
sharp teeth.

2.
tigers
_____
_____

3.
Tasmanian devils
_____
_____

4.
glass frogs
_____
_____

5.
Andean condors
_____
_____

6.
poodles
_____
_____

14 **Complete the dialogues with words from the box.**

because	Egyptian tortoises	habitat
How many	polar bears	red pandas
There are	There were	Why

1.

A: Why are ___red pandas___ endangered?

B: They're endangered _____ their _____ is disappearing.

2.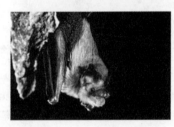

A: _____ bumblebee bats are there now?

B: _____ only about 200 left in the wild.

3.

A: How many _____ were there?

B: _____ over 50,000 in the wild.

4.

A: _____ are _____ endangered?

B: They're endangered because the climate is changing.

15 **Answer about you.**

Do you think it's important to help endangered animals? Explain.

_____

_____

_____

_____

unit 6

Life Long AGO

1 Listen and sing. Then match.

b.

Now there's TV.

a.

Now there's water from the tap.

In the Old Days

Life one hundred years ago
Was different, you see.
¹There were no computers,
²And there was no TV.

Life was different in the old days.
Life was different in so many ways.

³People got their water
From pumps or wells outdoors.
Now we just turn on the tap,
And out fresh water pours!

(Chorus)

Life was so much slower!
⁴Few people owned a car.
⁵Most kids had to walk to school,
And they walked pretty far!

(Chorus)

c.

Now there are computers.

e.

Now lots of people own cars.

d.

Now kids take a school bus.

2 Write about now and long ago.

Now

Long Ago

_____   _____

_____   _____

_____   _____

_____   _____

3 **Read and look at the pictures. Write the letter. Then trace the picture order.**

L drive cars

I traveled by horse and buggy

G used oil lamps

E listened to the radio

N use a microwave

O washed clothes by hand

L use a washing machine

G used a coal stove

A use electric lights

F watch TV

O use a cell phone

! used a phone with an operator

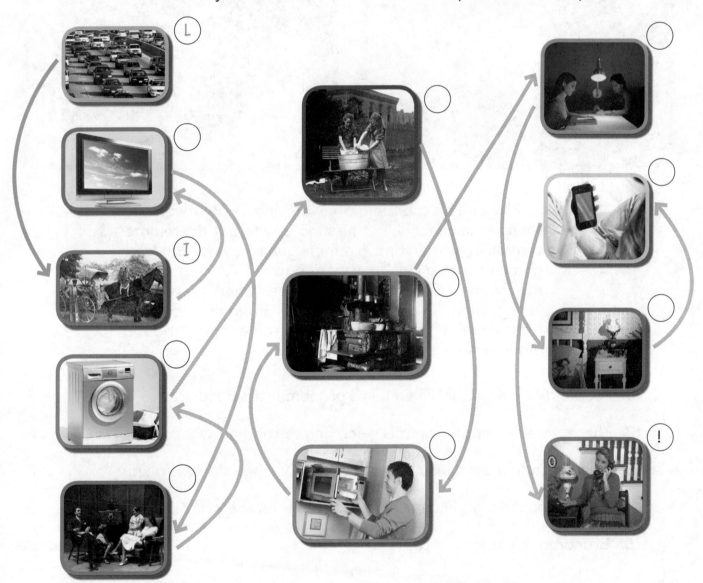

4 **Look at the letters in 3. Follow the picture order and write the letters. What do they spell?**

__L__ __I__ ___ ___ ___   ___ ___ ___ ___   ___ __G__ ___!

Story

5 **Read. Then circle *T* for *true* or *F* for *false*.**

Life Was Nicer Then

Billy and his grandma are watching TV. Billy wants to change the channel, but he's too lazy to get the remote control. They didn't have remote controls when Billy's grandma was a kid. They walked to the TV to change the channels. She thinks life was nicer when she was young. Then the microwave beeps. Grandma uses a microwave to make dinner. Maybe some things about modern life are nicer.

1. People didn't watch TV when Billy's grandma was a kid.   **T**   **F**

2. There were no remote controls when Billy's grandma was a kid.   **T**   **F**

3. Billy's grandma changed channels on the TV when she was a kid.   **T**   **F**

4. People cooked food in a microwave oven when she was a kid.   **T**   **F**

5. Grandma thinks life is nicer now.   **T**   **F**

6 **Answer about you.**

Is modern life nicer than life long ago? Explain.

_____

7 **Write the *now* and *long ago* activities.**

| use a computer | use a washing machine | use electric lights |
| used oil lamps | washed clothes by hand | wrote letters by hand |

a. _washed clothes_
   by hand ☐

b. _____
   _____ ☐

c. _____
   _____ ☐

d. _____
   _____ ☐

e. _____
   _____ ☐

f. _____
   _____ 1

8 **Look at 7. Listen for the activity. Number the pictures in the order you hear them.**

Grammar

Did people **have** cars in 1950?	Yes, they **did**.
Did people **have** cars in 1900?	No, they **didn't**. They traveled by horse and buggy or by train.

9 **Read and write the answers. Use *did* or *didn't*.**

1. **A:** Did your grandmother have a TV when she was young?

   B: ___Yes, she did___, but the shows were all in black and white.

2. **A:** Did people have cars fifty years ago?

   B: _____, but they were different. They used more gas then.

3. **A:** Did your grandfather play video games when he was a kid?

   B: _____ because people used to play other games then. They didn't have video games.

4. **A:** Did people have washing machines long ago?

   B: _____. They washed their clothes by hand in those days.

10 **Complete the questions and answers.**

1.

   A: _____ Grandma _____ a dog when she was young?

   B: _____, _____. She had a cute little dog.

2.

   A: _____ Mom _____ a cell phone in high school?

   B: _____, _____. She used public pay phones.

3.

   A: _____ Dad _____ a computer in school?

   B: _____, _____. He used a computer, but it was big and slow.

4.

   A: _____ Grandpa _____ emails when he was young?

   B: _____, _____. He wrote letters, not emails.

| Before TV, what **did** people **use to do** for entertainment at night? | They **used to listen** to the radio. |

11 **Complete the sentences.**

1. **A:** Before email, what _did people use to do_
   to communicate?
   B: They _used to write letters._

2. **A:** Before washing machines, what _____
   to wash clothes?
   B: They _____.

3. **A:** Before electricity, what _____
   for light?
   B: They _____.

4. **A:** Before TV, what _____
   for entertainment?
   B: They _____.

12 **Answer about you.**

1. Before you could read, what did you use to do?

   _____

2. Before you could walk, what did you use to do?

   _____

13 **Look in your house. What used to be different?**

   We used to have an old and slow computer. Now we have a new one.

   The bathroom used to be green. Now it's yellow.

1. _____

2. _____

Multiplication

14 **Read. Then complete the equations to solve the word problems.**

Horse and Buggy	**Model T**	**Modern Car**
A horse and buggy had an average speed of 8 miles per hour.	A Model T had an average speed of 25 miles per hour.	A modern car has an average speed of 56 miles per hour.

1. A horse and buggy travels for 10 hours. How far does it travel?

___8 mph___ X ___10___ = ___80___ miles
  average   number   distance
  speed   of hours   traveled

2. A horse and buggy travels for 8 hours. How far does it travel?

_____ X _____ = _____ miles

3. A Model T travels for 7 hours. How far does it travel?

_____ X _____ = _____ miles

4. A Model T travels for 6 hours. How far does it travel?

_____ X _____ = _____ miles

5. A modern car travels for 2 hours. How far does it travel?

_____ X _____ = _____ miles

6. A modern car travels for 3 hours. How far does it travel?

_____ X _____ = _____ miles

15 **Look at the answers in 14. Cross out the answers.**

4   25   64   8̶0̶   100   112   150   168   175

16 **Look at 15. Use the remaining numbers to make your own equation.**

A _____ travels for _____ hours. How far does it travel?

_____ X _____ = _____ miles

Quotation marks (" ") come in pairs. You put quotation marks around the words that people say.

"I had a great time at my grandpa's house," said Jaime.
"Did they watch TV back then?" he asked.
Miguel said, "I got a new cell phone for my birthday!"

17 **Write the sentences from the dialogues. Use *asked*, or *said* with quotation marks.**

How did people go places in 1905?

Did you use to ride a horse and buggy?

Ed   Mom

They used to ride a horse and buggy.

I'm not that old!

1. _"How did people go places in 1905?" Ed asked._

2. _____

3. _____

4. _____

18 **Look. What are they saying? Use *asked*, *said*, or *yelled* with quotation marks.**

1.

2.

19 **Listen to Jimmy and Maria. They are solving a problem. Match the questions with the answers.**

1. Define the problem.

What's Jimmy's problem?

2. Gather information.

What does his grandpa like?

3. Develop ideas.

What are some gift ideas?

4. Use the best idea.

Which idea does Jimmy choose?

5. Review and learn.

What did Jimmy learn at the party?

a. Maybe he'd like a book about the 1950s, tickets to a baseball game, or a book about Mickey Mantle.

b. He finds out that his grandpa likes Jackie Robinson and popcorn.

c. He is going to buy a book about Mickey Mantle.

d. He doesn't know what to buy for his grandpa's birthday.

e. He likes to watch baseball, read, and talk about the 1950s.

20 **Solve a problem at home.**

Think about a problem you have at home. Here are some ideas:

I need to organize my video games.

I don't have time to do my homework.

I have to save water.

I'm bored.

Now follow the steps to solve the problem.

1. Define the problem. _____

_____

2. Gather information. _____

_____

3. Develop ideas. _____

_____

4. Use the best idea. _____

_____

5. Review and learn. _____

_____

21 **Circle the correct words. Write the answers.**

1. **A: Did / Do** people have microwave ovens 100 years ago?

   B: _____

2. **A:** Did your city or town **had / have** cars ten years ago?

   B: _____

3. **A:** Did people **use to / used to** write emails before electricity?

   B: _____

4. **A: Did / Do** people use cell phones to talk now?

   B: _____

22 **Look. Find four things that didn't exist long ago. Circle and write.**

1. ___They didn't use to have computers._____

2. _____

3. _____

4. _____

Think Big

1 Look at Units 4, 5, and 6. Choose words from the units. Write them in the charts.

2 Choose and draw one path. Gather information, and add your own information.

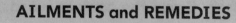

AILMENTS and REMEDIES

headache	rest

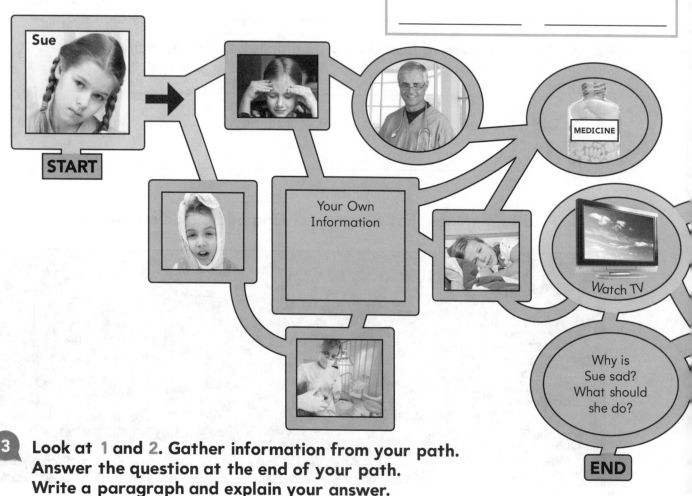

Sue
START

Your Own Information

MEDICINE

Watch TV

Why is Sue sad? What should she do?

END

3 Look at 1 and 2. Gather information from your path. Answer the question at the end of your path. Write a paragraph and explain your answer.

_____

_____

_____

_____

_____

_____

ENDANGERED ANIMALS	TECHNOLOGY NOW
tigers	television
_____	_____
_____	_____
_____	_____

Endangered Animals

TIGERS:
Used to be
100,000.
Now 3200!

KOMODO
DRAGON:
Used to be
20,000.
Now 5000!

END

Why
are they
endangered?
What should
we do?

Long Ago
and Now

Your Own
Information

END

What did
people use?
What do they
use now?

 In Your Classroom

Work in a group and share.

unit 7 Special DAYS

20

1 **Listen and write the words.**

♪ **Special Days Are Fun!** ♪

This Friday is a special day—
The ¹_____.
We're going to stay up very late.
At ²_____ we're going to cheer!

Special days are cool. Special days are fun.
Special days bring special treats for everyone!

Every ³_____,
We celebrate and say,
"Happy New Year!" to everyone
Because it's ⁴_____.

(Chorus)

There are lots of special days,
And each one is a treat.
We have ⁵_____ and
⁶_____ and delicious food to eat.

fireworks
January first
last day of the year
midnight
New Year's Day
parades

2 **Look at the song in 1. Check (✓) the correct box.**

1. This Friday is

☐ December 30th.   ☐ December 31st.   ☐ January 1st.

2. They are going to cheer

☐ in the middle of the night.   ☐ in the middle of the day.   ☐ all day and all night.

3. The night before New Year's Day they

☐ stay up late.   ☐ go to bed early.   ☐ sleep late.

3 **Look. Answer the questions with a complete sentence.**

Special Day	Who	Things They Do
Earth Day	Jenny Emilio	watch a parade plant a tree
Birthday	Tony Karen	have a party and my friends give me presents go to the movies
Independence Day	Jenny Karen	watch fireworks and eat special foods see my cousins
Valentine's Day	Tony Emilio	eat chocolate give my mom flowers

1. What does Emilio do on Earth Day? _____

2. What does Karen do on her birthday? _____

3. Jenny watches fireworks on what special day? _____

4. What does Tony do on Valentine's Day? _____

5. Jenny watches a parade on what special day? _____

6. Tony has a party on what special day? _____

7. What does Karen do on Independence Day? _____

8. Emilio gives his mom flowers on what special day? _____

4 **Read. Answer the questions with complete sentences.**

The Anniversary Party

Gwen knows her parents' anniversary is on the tenth. Gwen plans a big celebration for their anniversary on June 10th. They're going out for a special dinner. She's making a cake. Her parents like the plans, but there's a problem. Their anniversary is on *July* 10th, not June 10th.

1. Gwen is planning a big celebration. What's the special day?

_____

2. What does Gwen plan for the celebration?

_____

3. Do her parents like the plans?

_____

4. What's the problem?

_____

5. What should they do?

_____

5 Listen and match.

Dad's birthday

Sister's birthday

go to a parade

Dad's party/give presents

FEBRUARY

SUNDAY	MONDAY	TUESDAY	WEDNESDAY	THURSDAY	FRIDAY	SATURDAY
					1	2
3	4	5	6	7	8	9
10	11	12	13	14	15	16
17	18	19	20	21	22	23
24	25	26	27	28		

Mom's special dinner

Sister's party

Grandparents' anniversary

Mom's birthday

Valentine's Day

6 Look at the calendar in **5**. Write the dates and special days.

1. _____

_____

2. _____

_____

3. _____

_____

Grammar

Are you/they going to visit Grandma **on the ninth**?	Yes, **on the ninth**.
Is he/she going to visit Grandma **on the fifth**?	No, **on the ninth**.

7 **Read and cross out the letters. Use the remaining letters to write the special days.**

1. Cross out the first, third, fifth, ninth, tenth, twelfth, and fourteenth letters.

G̶ E T̶ A B̶ R T H I̶ N̶ D O̶ A M̶ Y

_E_ _A_ _R_ _T_ _H_   _D_ _A_ _Y_

2. Cross out the first, third, seventh, tenth, thirteenth, sixteenth, seventeenth, and twentieth letters.

B V I A L E R N T H I N P E S Y N D A O Y

__ __ __ __ __ __ __ __ __'__ __ __ __ __

3. Cross out the second, fourth, sixth, seventh, ninth, eleventh, sixteenth, seventeenth, and nineteenth letters.

N A E H W P V Y I E N A R S D E V A E Y

__ __ __ __ __ __ __'__ __ __ __ __

8 **Read and write the answer.**

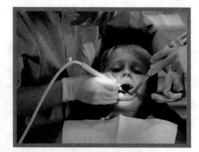

Sam has to go to the dentist on the ninth of March. It is a regular checkup and cleaning. On the fifteenth of March, he is going to have his birthday party. His cousins can't come. So on the twentieth of March, he is going to visit his cousins. They are going to go to the movies.

1. When is Sam going to celebrate his birthday? _____

2. When is Sam going to visit his cousins? _____

3. When is Sam going to have his teeth cleaned? _____

When **are**	you	**going to have** the party?	I	**am going to have** it on Monday.
	they		We	**are going to have** it on Monday.
			They	
When **is**	he / she	**going to visit** Grandma?	He / She	**is going to visit** her next month.

9 **Answer the questions about Sarah's calendar.**

MAY

Sun	Mon	Tue	Wed	Thu	Fri	Sat
1	**2**	**3** Today	**4**	**5**	**6**	**7** Birthday party
8	**9**	**10**	**11** Parents' anniversary	**12**	**13**	**14** Sister visits friend
15	**16**	**17**	**18** Watch parade	**19**	**20**	**21** Watch fireworks
22	**23**	**24**	**25**	**26**	**27** Uncle Joe visits	**28**
29	**30**	**31**				

1. When is Sarah going to have her birthday party?

She is going to have it on Saturday, the seventh.

2. When are her parents going to celebrate their anniversary?

_____

3. When is her sister going to visit her friend?

_____

4. Is she going to watch the parade on the 17th?

_____

5. Are they going to watch the fireworks on Sunday?

_____

Leap Year

10 **Read about leap years.**

We usually say a year is 365 days long, because that's about the time it takes for Earth to travel around the sun. It actually takes 365 days, 5 hours, 49 minutes, and 12 seconds. The extra 5 hours, 49 minutes, and 12 seconds add up to an extra day every four years on February 29. This day is called *leap day*. Years with the extra day are called *leap years*. They can be divided evenly by four. For example, 2004, 2008, and 2012 were leap years.

11 **Write the answers.**

1. How long does it take Earth to travel around the sun?

_____ days

_____ hours

_____ minutes

_____ seconds

2. How many days are there in a leap year? _____

12 **Solve these problems.**

1. Billy was born on February 29, 2000. Write the next four years he can celebrate his birthday on February 29.

_____ _____ _____ _____

2. It's February 29, 2012. It's Jessi's birthday. Write the next four years she can celebrate her birthday on February 29.

_____ _____ _____ _____

Unusual Festivals

13 **Read. Circle _T_ for _true_ or _F_ for _false_.**

> **Holi—The Festival of Colors**
> This festival takes place every spring to celebrate the end of winter and the arrival of spring. It is celebrated in India, Nepal, and other places. During Holi, people throw colored powder and water at each other.
>
> **Tomatina—The Tomato Festival**
> Every year, on the last Wednesday of August, there is a messy festival in Buñol, Spain. People run around throwing red tomatoes at each other.
>
> **The Monkey Buffet**
> On the last weekend in November, the people of Lopburi, Thailand, invite hundreds of monkeys to a feast of peanuts, fruit, and vegetables.
>
> **Qoyllurit'i—Festival of the Snows**
> Every May on a glacier in Peru, people celebrate with music and dancing for three days and nights. Everyone leaves together carrying torches.

1. In the Festival of Colors, people swim in colored water.   T   F

2. In the Monkey Buffet, monkeys throw peanuts.   T   F

3. In Festival of the Snows, there is silence.   T   F

4. The Tomato Festival is very clean.   T   F

14 **Write about you.**

1. You are going to Tomatina. What are you going to bring?

_____

_____

2. You are going to Qoyllurit'i. What are you going to bring?

_____

_____

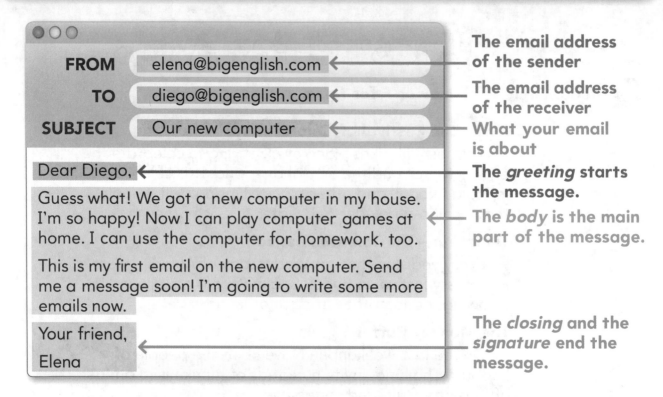

FROM elena@bigenglish.com — The email address of the sender

TO diego@bigenglish.com — The email address of the receiver

SUBJECT Our new computer — What your email is about

Dear Diego, — The *greeting* starts the message.

Guess what! We got a new computer in my house. I'm so happy! Now I can play computer games at home. I can use the computer for homework, too. — The *body* is the main part of the message.

This is my first email on the new computer. Send me a message soon! I'm going to write some more emails now.

Your friend, — The *closing* and the *signature* end the message.

Elena

15 **Write an email to a friend. Invite your friend to a celebration.**

fireworks   New Year's Day   your birthday party

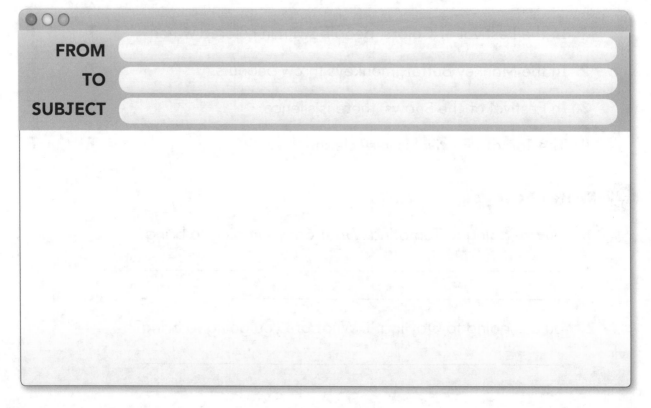

FROM

TO

SUBJECT

16 **Look at the pictures. Answer the questions.**

FEBRUARY 14

MARCH 10

APRIL 22

JULY 4

NOVEMBER 1

DECEMBER 31

1. When are we going to celebrate their 50th anniversary?

On November first

2. When are they going to celebrate Earth Day?

_____

3. When is he going to watch the fireworks?

_____

4. Are you going to a parade on July 5th?

_____

5. Is she going to have her birthday party on March 10th?

_____

6. Are they going to have a Valentine's Day party on February 9th?

_____

17 **Look at 16. Number the activities in calendar order. Write the special day.**

a. ☐ watch fireworks _____

b. 1 get and give cards _____

c. ☐ watch a parade _____

1 Listen. Answer the questions. Write full sentences.

The Best and the Worst

Matthew collects toy cars—
He has one hundred and seven.
But Pam's collection is bigger;
She has three hundred and eleven!

May is good at playing games;
She's really good at chess.
But Paul is even better than May.
And Liz, well, she's the best!

What's your hobby, Bobby?
What do you like to do?
What's your hobby, Bobby?
What is fun for you?

Steve is a terrible singer.
Emma's worse than Steve.
But David's singing is the worst.
When he sings, people leave!

It's good to have a hobby.
Some people have a few.
Even if you're not the best,
It still is fun to do!

(Chorus)

1. Who sings the worst?

_____

2. Who is the best at playing chess?

_____

3. Who collects the most toy cars?

_____

4. How many toy cars are in the biggest collection?

_____

2 **Draw the path. Connect the pictures in this order:**

soccer player → painter → toy car collection → chess player →
coin collection → singer → video game player → shell collection →
doll collection → dancer → basketball player → writer

3 **Look at 2. Color the letters on the correct path.**

4 **Complete the question. Use the letters in 2. Then write the answer.**

What I___ ___ ___ ___ ___ ___ ___ ___ ___?

_____.

Story

5 **Read. Then circle T for *true* or F for *false*.**

The School Play

Megan's dad is excited about this year's school play. The play is *Snow White*. He wants Megan to be a star in the play. He wants her to be an important character like Snow White or the Evil Queen, but her friends Lizzie and Abby have those parts. Megan is going to be a tree. It's a small part, but Megan's dad is very proud of her.

1. Megan is going to be in the play *Snow White*.	T	F
2. Megan's dad thinks the play is boring.	T	F
3. Megan's dad wants her to be a star in the play.	T	F
4. Megan is going to be a tree.	T	F
5. The tree is the star of the play.	T	F
6. Megan's dad is sad because she's not the star.	T	F

6 **Write about you.**

1. What do you like to do?

_____

2. What character would you want to be in *Snow White*?

_____

3. What are you good at?

_____

7 **Listen and match.**

1. Susan's team is

2. Cassie's story is

3. Grandpa used to be

4. Diane is

5. Jason has

6. The doll from Russia is

a. the best painter.

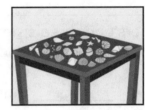

b. the biggest shell collection.

c. the longest story.

d. the oldest in her collection.

e. the best in town.

f. the worst video game player.

Grammar

> Chris has a **big** stamp collection.
>
> Katie's collection is **bigger** than Chris's collection.
>
> Kyle has **the biggest** stamp collection.

8 **Read. Then use a form of *big* or *old* to complete each sentence.**

> Philip has two brothers and three sisters. Pablo has three brothers and four sisters. Tony has two brothers and two sisters.

1. Philip's family is _____ than Tony's.

2. Pablo's family is the _____ of all.

3. Tony's family is _____.

> Dean's grandma is eighty-six years old. Betty's grandma is seventy-four years old. Harriet's grandma is ninety-one years old.

4. Dean's grandma is _____ than Betty's grandma.

5. Betty's grandma is _____.

6. Harriet's grandma is the _____ of all.

9 **Look at the pictures. Write sentences using the words.**

Pam	Sue	Mae

1. _____ (older)

2. _____ (oldest)

Laura is a **good** soccer player.	My brother's paintings are **bad**.
Steve is a **better** player **than** Laura.	My sister's paintings are **worse than** his.
Yoko is **the best** soccer player in the class.	My paintings are **the worst** of all.

10 Listen. Write and add the scores. Compare the scores and complete the sentences.

INDIVIDUAL SCORES

1. Tony's score

   $7 + 7 + 8 = 22$

2. Molly's score

   _____

3. Rob's score

   _____

FINAL RESULTS

4. Tony is a good singer, but Rob is _____ .

5. Rob is a _____ singer _____ Tony.

6. Molly is _____ singer of all and the Next Big Star!

Hobbies Are Good for You

11 **Answer the questions. Write complete sentences.**

1. How can a hobby make you be more creative?

   _____

2. How can a hobby help you learn?

   _____

3. How can a hobby help you build skills?

   _____

4. How can a hobby motivate you?

   _____

12 **Answer about your hobbies. Write complete sentences.**

1. What are your hobbies?

   _____

2. Would you like to try a new hobby? Explain.

   _____

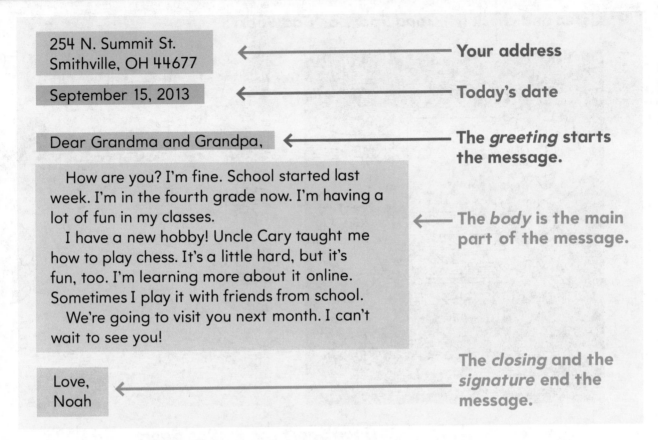

254 N. Summit St.
Smithville, OH 44677 ← Your address

September 15, 2013 ← Today's date

Dear Grandma and Grandpa, ← The *greeting* starts the message.

How are you? I'm fine. School started last week. I'm in the fourth grade now. I'm having a lot of fun in my classes.

I have a new hobby! Uncle Cary taught me how to play chess. It's a little hard, but it's fun, too. I'm learning more about it online. Sometimes I play it with friends from school.

← The *body* is the main part of the message.

We're going to visit you next month. I can't wait to see you!

Love,
Noah

The *closing* and the *signature* end the message.

13 **Write an informal letter to a friend. Tell your friend about a hobby. Here are some ideas:**

a healthy hobby   a creative hobby   a hobby that helps you learn

_____

_____

_____

_____

_____

_____

_____

_____

_____

_____

_____

14 Listen and check (✓) *Good Sport* or *Bad Sport*.

	Good Sport	**Bad Sport**
1. a. Mark is a	☐	☐
b. Stephen is a	☐	☐
2. a. Wendy is a	☐	☐
b. Liam is a	☐	☐
3. a. Dina is a	☐	☐
b. Sally is a	☐	☐
4. a. Harry is a	☐	☐
b. Derek is a	☐	☐

15 Write sentences about a *good sport* and sentences about a *bad sport*.

1. Good Sport: _____

_____

2. Bad Sport: _____

_____

16 Complete the dialogues with forms of *bad*, *good*, *old*, and *new*.

1.

A: Carol is ___bad___ at chess.

B: Yes. But Henry is _____ than Carol.

A: That's true. But I'm _____ of all.

2.

A: Sean is a _____ singer.

B: I know! But Chris is _____ than Sean.

A: Yes. But Brian is _____ singer of all.

3.

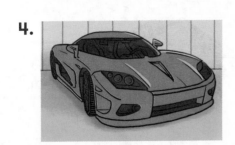

A: Patty's grandma is 80. That's _____.

B: Yes. But Marge's grandma is _____. She's 85.

A: I know. And Randy's grandma is _____ of all. She's 95.

4.

A: My dad got a car a few weeks ago. It's red and shiny and _____.

B: Oh yeah, well my dad got a car last week. It's _____ than your dad's car.

A: Well, maybe. But my friend's dad has a new car. It's _____ of all. He got his car yesterday!

17 Answer about your family. Write complete sentences.

1. Who is the best singer? _____

2. Who is the worst singer? _____

3. Who is the best dancer? _____

4. Who is the worst dancer? _____

5. Who is the oldest person? _____

unit 9

Learning New THINGS

1 **Listen and write the words in the song.**

> bake   draw   learn   show
> sing   skateboard speak

Learning Is Fun

Do you know how to ¹_____?
It's so awesome. It's so cool!
I can ²_____ you how to do it
On Friday after school.

It's fun to learn new things,
Like how to ³_____,
or ⁴_____, or ⁵_____!
I wish I had lots more free time.
I would try to ⁶_____ everything!

I'd like to learn to speak English.
"It's hard!" my friends all say.
But I think it's really interesting.
I'd like to ⁷_____ it well one day.

(Chorus)

Do you want to learn English?

Sure!

2 **Do you want to learn new things? What do you want to learn? Write the answer.**

_____

_____

_____

3 **Solve the puzzle. Write the words below and in the boxes**

Across →

1.

___sing___ like a
rock star

2.

draw _____
books

3.

_____

4.

make a

_____

Down ↓

5.

_____
a cake

6.

build a

_____

7.

play the

_____

8.

_____ like a
hip-hop artist

4 **What activities are *amazing*, *dangerous*, and *difficult*? Write.**

1. I think it's amazing to _____.

2. I think it's dangerous to _____.

3. I think it's difficult to _____.

Story

5 **Read. Circle *T* for *true* or *F* for *false*.**

The Best in the Class

$4+2+1=$

BUS STOP

Kit and her brother Stan are at the bus stop. They see Gerald, a boy from Kit's class. Kit thinks Gerald is really smart because he can do many things. He's good at math and science. He can speak several languages and play the piano. He draws comic books, and he made his own website. But Gerald spills his drink all over. Maybe Gerald isn't smart about *everything*.

1. Gerald is in Stan's class.   T   F

2. Gerald is good at science and math.   T   F

3. Gerald can speak more than one language.   T   F

4. Gerald can play the piano.   T   F

5. Gerald can drive a bus.   T   F

6. Gerald can open his drink neatly.   T   F

6 **What happens next in the story? Write. Here are some ideas.**

Gerald starts speaking Spanish to the man at the bus stop.

Kit and Stan say "hi" to Gerald and share funny comic books.

Gerald drops his bag and a talking robot walks out.

_____

_____

_____

7 **Listen. Write the answers in complete sentences.**

1.

Does Bobby want to learn how to skateboard? Why or why not?

_____

_____

_____

2.

Does Tommy want to learn how to dance hip-hop? Why or why not?

_____

_____

_____

3.

Does Diana want to learn how to play tennis? Why or why not?

_____

_____

_____

4.

Does Erik want to learn how to bake a cake? Why or why not?

_____

_____

_____

Grammar

Do you **know how to play** the piano?			Yes, I do. / No, I don't.	
What would	you	like to learn?	I'd	like to **learn how to play** the piano.
	he/she		He'd/She'd	
	they		They'd	

8 **Answer the questions in complete sentences.**

1. What would she like to learn?

_____

_____

2. What would he like to learn?

_____

_____

3. What would they like to learn?

_____

_____

4. What would she like to learn?

_____

_____

What **do**	you	**think of** tennis?	I	**think** it's a lot of fun.
	they		We	
			They	
What **does**	he/she	**think of** ballet?	He/She	**thinks** it's boring.

9 **Look and answer.**

1. What does he think of the movie?

_____

2. What does she think of the zoo?

_____

10 **Look at the school notice. Answer the questions in complete sentences.**

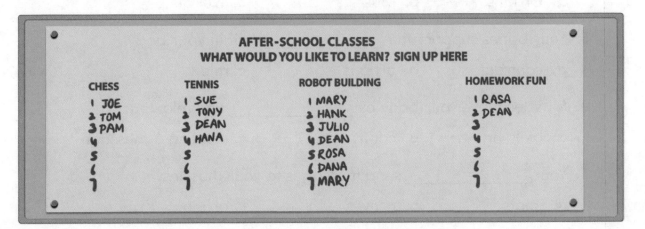

AFTER-SCHOOL CLASSES
WHAT WOULD YOU LIKE TO LEARN? SIGN UP HERE

CHESS
1 JOE
2 TOM
3 PAM
4
5
6
7

TENNIS
1 SUE
2 TONY
3 DEAN
4 HANA
5
6
7

ROBOT BUILDING
1 MARY
2 HANK
3 JULIO
4 DEAN
5 ROSA
6 DANA
7 MARY

HOMEWORK FUN
1 RASA
2 DEAN
3
4
5
6
7

1. What would Joe and Pam like to learn?

_____

2. What would Hana like to learn?

_____

3. What class is the most fun?

_____

4. What would you like to learn?

_____

5. What do you think of *Homework Fun*?

_____

6. Do you know how to play chess?

_____

11 **Number the sentences in the correct order.**

Moving Your Body

_____ Her muscles contract, and she hits the ball.

_____ The tennis player decides to hit the ball.

_____ Her nerves send a message to her muscles.

_____ Her brain tells her nerves that she wants to hit the ball.

12 **Complete the sentences. Circle the correct words.**

1. Muscles, _____, and joints are the three main parts of your body's musculoskeletal system.

   a. bones   **b.** nerves   **c.** organs

2. _____ pull your bones in different directions so your body moves.

   a. Organs   **b.** Muscles   **c.** Nerves

3. Your bones support the _____ within your body.

   a. contract   **b.** organs   **c.** relax

4. Muscles move your body by _____ and relaxing.

   a. building   **b.** contracting   **c.** sending a message

5. Your _____ send messages to your muscles.

   a. joints   **b.** nerves   **c.** organs

6. Your _____ connect two or more bones to each other.

   a. joints   **b.** muscles   **c.** nerves

7. Your _____ are your body's frame.

   a. bones   **b.** joints   **c.** muscles

8. When your muscles contract, they get shorter. When they _____, they get longer.

   a. contract   **b.** relax   **c.** send messages

13 **Read about Yuto Miyazawa.**

Yuto Miyazawa was a professional musician when he was only eight years old!

He is in the Guinness Book of World Records as "The Youngest Professional Guitarist." He has been on TV and performed at Madison Square Garden. He even played with famous musicians like Ozzy Osbourne, Les Paul, and G.E. Smith.

14 **What would Yuto Miyazawa say? Imagine and write.**

1. Would you like to learn to play another instrument?

Yuto: _____

2. Do you always like playing the guitar?

Yuto: _____

3. What do you think of playing with famous musicians?

Yuto: _____

15 **Now write about you. Explain your answer.**

1. Would you like to learn to play the guitar?

_____

2. By sixteen, Gregory Smith had several college degrees and traveled the world helping young people. Would you like to be like Gregory Smith?

_____

3. What do you think of these extraordinary kids?

_____

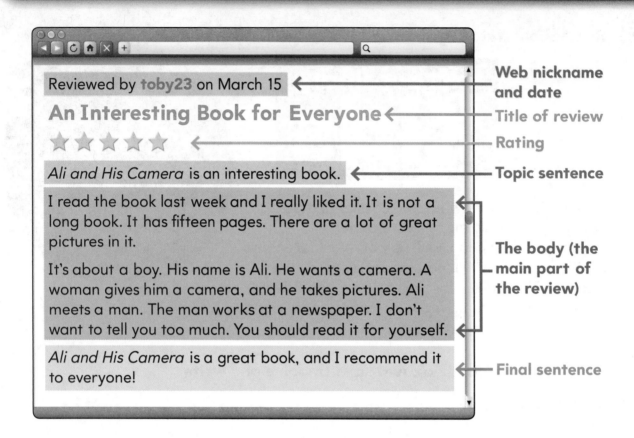

Reviewed by **toby23** on March 15 ← Web nickname and date

An Interesting Book for Everyone ← Title of review

★ ★ ★ ★ ★ ← Rating

Ali and His Camera is an interesting book. ← Topic sentence

I read the book last week and I really liked it. It is not a long book. It has fifteen pages. There are a lot of great pictures in it.

It's about a boy. His name is Ali. He wants a camera. A woman gives him a camera, and he takes pictures. Ali meets a man. The man works at a newspaper. I don't want to tell you too much. You should read it for yourself. ← The body (the main part of the review)

Ali and His Camera is a great book, and I recommend it to everyone! ← Final sentence

16 **Write a review of a TV show or website you like.**

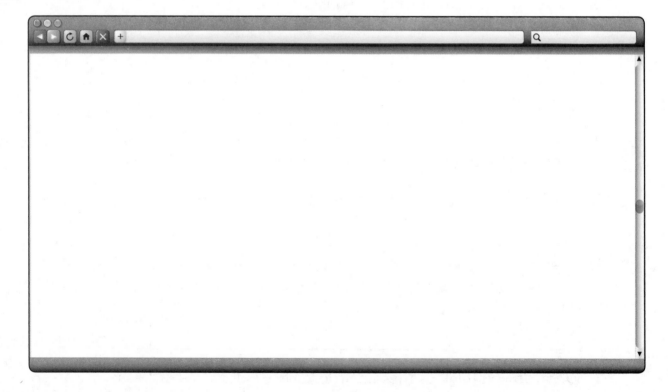

17 **Look at the chart. Write questions and answers.**

What do you think of . . . ?				
Luisa	interesting	dangerous	cool	boring
Martin	difficult	amazing	boring	fun

1. What does Luisa think of drawing comic books?

She thinks it's boring.

2. _____

She thinks it's interesting.

3. What does Martin think of singing like a rock star?

_____

4. _____

He thinks it's amazing.

18 **Answer the questions in complete sentences.**

1. Does Karen know how to play the guitar? *(no)*

_____

2. Does Phil know how to speak Chinese? *(yes)*

_____

3. What would she like to learn? *(build a robot)*

_____

4. What do they want to learn? *(dance like a hip-hop artist)*

_____

Think Big

1 **Think Big. Make guesses about Ben. Check (✓) the answers.**

Look at the happy and sad faces on Ben's calendar. Ben thinks some days are the best. He thinks some days are the worst.

1. What is Ben like?

   ☐ friendly ☐ funny

   ☐ good at music ☐ good at sports

   ☐ serious ☐ smart

2. What would Ben like to do?

   ☐ have a party ☐ learn to play baseball

   ☐ learn to play the guitar ☐ play video games

   ☐ watch fireworks ☐ watch TV

Sun	Mon
31 Dec. NEW YEAR'S EVE ☺ ☺ ☺	**1** Jan. ?
7 LEARN HOW TO ☹ ☹ ☹	**8** MEET FRIENDS SHARE COLLECTION ☺ ☺

2 **Think Big. Write on Ben's calendar. Write a hobby or things for Ben to learn on the tenth and the thirteenth.**

Make a guess about these two days.

3 **Think Big. Look at the calendar. Make guesses and write the answers.**

1. What's Ben going to do on Monday?

   _____

2. What special day is on Saturday, the sixth?

   _____

BEN'S CALENDAR

Tues	Wed	Thurs	Fri	Sat
 **2** MEET FRIENDS	**3** PRACTICE PIANO	**4** LEARN TO PLAY 	**5** BAKE MOM'S BIRTHDAY CAKE	**6** ?
SHARE COLLECTION 😐 😐	☹ ☹	😊 😊 😊	😊 😊 😊	
9 PRACTICE SOCCER	**10** ? _____	**11** MAKE A WEBSITE 	**12** LEARN TO PLAY DRUMS	**13** ? _____
☹ ☹ ☹ *The best!*	😊 😊 😊	😊 😊 😊	☹ ☹ *The worst!*	☹ ☹ ☹

4 **What do you think of Ben? Would you like to be Ben's friend? Write a letter about Ben to your parents. Begin:**

Dear Mom and Dad,

   I have a new classmate. His name is Ben. _____

_____

_____

_____

_____

_____

_____

5 **In Your Classroom**

Work in a group and share.

Who is **bigger**, Chris or Tom?	Chris is **bigger than** Tom.

old	→	old**er**
big	→	big**ger**
heavy	→	heav**ier**

1 **Read. Write the answers.**

1. What is bigger? An elephant or an ant?

   An elephant is _____ an ant.

2. What is heavier? A notebook or a computer?

   A computer is _____ a notebook.

3. Who is older? Your grandmother or your aunt?

   _____

4. Who is taller? Your mother or your father?

   _____

5. What is smaller? A baseball or a basketball?

   _____

My sister's hair is longer than **my hair**.	My sister's hair is longer than **mine**.
My sister's hair is longer than **your hair**.	My sister's hair is longer than **yours**.

2 **Circle the correct word.**

1. **Your / Yours** backpack is heavy. But my backpack is heavier than **your / yours**.

2. **Their / Theirs** hair is long. But my hair is longer than **their / theirs**.

3. **Her / Hers** brother is younger than **my / mine**.

4. **Our / Ours** classroom is bigger than **their / theirs** classroom.

5. **My / Mine** friend is taller than Shaun's.

| **Where** is | he/she | going after school? | He/She | is going to soccer practice. |
| **What** are | you | doing tonight? | We | are watching a movie at home. |

1 **Look. Write *What* or *Where*. Answer the questions.**

walk the dog

visit the dentist

1. _____ is she doing after school today?

   She _____.

2. _____ are they going on Saturday?

   They _____.

play computer games

go to the mall

3. _____ is he doing tonight?

   He _____.

4. _____ are you going tonight?

   We _____.

| **How often** does | he/she | have guitar lessons? | **How often** do | you/they | go to school? |

2 **Circle the correct question. Write the answer.**

1. **How often do / How often does** they wash the dishes?

| Mon | Tues |

   _____ a week.

2. **How often do / How often does** she feed the birds?

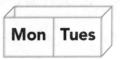

| Sun |

   _____ a week.

What **would** you **like**?			**I'd like** some soup.		I'd like → I would like
What would	he/she	**like**?	He'**d**/She'**d**	**like** yogurt.	He'd/She'd like → He/She would like

1 **Look. Write questions. Write the answers.**

1. What would she like for breakfast?

_____ bacon and eggs.

2. What _____ for a snack?

_____.

3. _____ for dessert?

_____.

> ### Favorite Food Survey
> **1. Stacy:** bacon and eggs for breakfast
> **2. Martin:** steamed buns for a snack
> **3. Stacy and Martin:** yogurt and fruit for dessert

Would	you he/she they	**like to try** some curry?	**Yes,**	I we he/she they	**would.**	**No,**	I we he/she they	**wouldn't.**

2 **Complete the dialogue. Use *does*, *do*, *don't*, *would*, *wouldn't*, or *like*.**

1. A: Does Paula like spicy food?

B: Yes, _____.

A: _____ she _____ to try some chili?

B: Yes, she would. She loves chili.

2. A: Do you like sour things?

B: No, _____.

A: Would you like to try some lemonade?

B: No, _____. Thanks anyway.

I			I		
You			You		
He/She	**should** eat healthy foods.		He/She	**shouldn't** stay up late.	
We			We		
They			They		

1 **Write sentences with *should* and *shouldn't*. Use the ideas in the box.**

1. I have a fever.

    You shouldn't go to school today.

    You should rest.

go to school today
rest

2. Her tooth hurts.

    _____

    _____

go to the dentist
eat so many sweets

3. Ted fell and hurt his knee.

    _____

    _____

go to soccer practice
see the school nurse

4. Some children always feel tired.

    _____

    _____

watch so much TV
get more exercise

I		**myself.**
You		**yourself.**
He/She	should take care of	**himself/herself.**
We		**ourselves.**
They		**themselves.**

2 **Look at 1. Complete the sentences. Use *herself*, *himself*, *themselves*, or *yourself*.**

1. You have to take care of _____.

2. She has to take care of _____.

3. He _____.

4. They _____.

| How many chimpanzees were there 100 years ago? | There **were** more than one million. But now there **are** only about 200,000. |

1 Complete the sentences with *how many*, *there are*, *there were* or *are there*, *were there*.

Animal	Habitat	Population in the Past	Population Now
Mexican walking fish	streams and rivers in Mexico	a lot	almost none

_____ Mexican walking fish _____ in Mexico now?

_____ a lot of Mexican walking fish in Mexican streams and

rivers in the past?

Now, _____ almost none. In the past, _____ a lot.

| Why are chimpanzees endangered? | They're endangered **because** people are moving into their habitat. |

2 Answer the questions. Use the information in the box and *because*.

> people are killing them for their fur
> people are keeping them as pets

1. Why is the Egyptian tortoise endangered?

   It is endangered _____

   _____.

2. Why are tigers endangered?

   _____

   _____.

Did people **have** cars in 1950?	Yes, they **did**.
Did people **have** cars in 1900?	No, they **didn't**. They traveled by horse and buggy or by train.
Before TV, what **did** people **use to do** for entertainment at night?	They **used to listen** to the radio.

 1 **Read. Then answer the questions. Use *did* or *didn't*, *do* or *don't*, *use* or *used*.**

Then and Now

1930's – People usually listened to the radio. They didn't own TVs.

Today – People sometimes listen to the radio. Most people watch TV.

1950's – People wrote letters by hand.

Today – Many people write letters on the computer.

1970's – Young people played outdoor games, like hide and seek, or tag.

Today – Many people, young and old, play video games.

1. Did people listen to the radio years ago?

Yes, _____ because they didn't have TVs.

Do people listen to the radio now?

Yes, _____, but they usually watch TV.

2. Did people use to write letters on the computer a long time ago?

_____

Do they write letters on the computer now?

_____

3. Before video games, what _____ young people

_____ to do for fun?

They _____ to play hide and seek, or tag outdoors.

When **are**	you	going to have the party?	I	am going to have it on Monday.
	they		we	are going to have it on Monday.
When **is**	he/she	going to visit Grandma?	They	
			He/She	is going to visit her next month.
Are you/they going to visit Grandma **on the ninth**?			Yes, **on the ninth**.	
Is he/she going to visit Grandma **on the fifth**?			No, **on the ninth**.	

1 Complete the questions and write the answers. Use *going to* and words from the box.

> fourth   second   third   twenty-first

1.

(See the dentist July 2)

When _____ he

_____ the dentist?

On the _____ *second* _____.

2.

(Go on vacation July 3)

When _____ they

_____ on vacation?

_____.

3.

(Watch fireworks July 4)

When _____ you

_____ fireworks?

_____.

4.

(Have a party July 21)

When _____ you

_____ a party?

_____.

Chris has a **big** stamp collection.	My brother's paintings are **bad**.
Katie's collection is **bigger** than Chris's collection.	My sister's paintings are **worse than** his.
Kyle has **the biggest** stamp collection.	My paintings are **the worst** of all.

1 **Complete the sentences. Use a form of the word in parentheses.**

1. (loud)

Many musical instruments are loud. A flute can make
a loud sound. A trumpet is _____ than a flute.
But a drum is the _____ of all three.

2. (weird)

There are many weird looking wild animals. I think a
coconut crab is very weird, but a whistling spider is
_____. The _____ of all is the tarsier.

3. (bad)

	Losses
The Bears	5
The Tigers	3
The Lions	4

The Bears, Tigers and Lions are popular baseball teams, but
they are not having a good year. The Bears team is _____
of the three this year. The Lions are _____ than the Tigers.
But the Tigers are pretty _____, too.

Do you **know how to play** the piano?			Yes, I do. / No, I don't.	
What would	you	going to have the party?	I'd	like to **learn how to play** the piano.
	he/she		He'd/She'd	
	they		They'd	

1 **Complete the dialogues.**

1. **A:** Do you _____

_____?

B: _____. I skateboard every day after school. I think it's cool.

2. **A:** Does she _____

_____?

B: _____. But she'd like to learn how to play. She thinks it's a lot of fun.

2 **Read. Then answer the questions. Use the words in the box.**

> bake a cake   make a website   sing like a rock star

1. Jeff and Tina are going to take singing lessons next semester. What would they like to learn?

   _____.

2. Sue loves cakes. She's taking a baking class now. What would she like to learn?

   _____.

3. Bryan loves computers. He is taking a web-design class now. What would he like to learn?

   _____.

My BIG ENGLISH World

Workbook 4

My name: _____

My age: _____

My address: _____

My family: _____

ME →

ENGLISH
AROUND ME

Look around you. Paste or draw things with English words. Write everyday words and sentences.

Everyday Words

Everyday Sentences

Henry's Chocolate

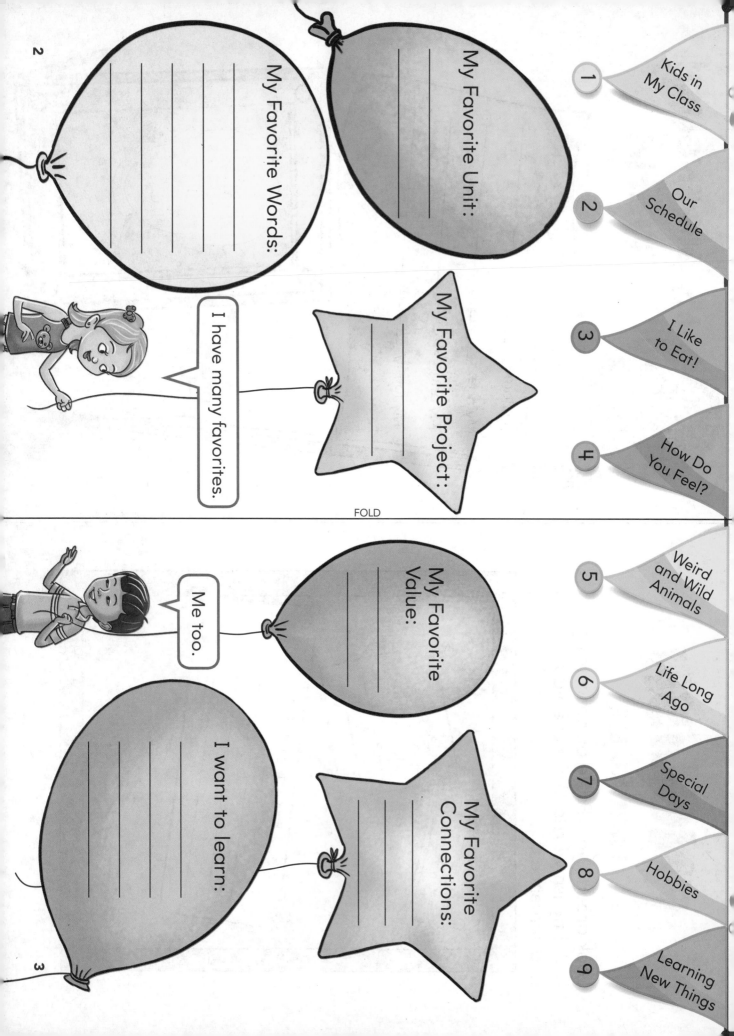